"The Raphael Cross Cultu
needed area in the practice
clinicians with an integratec
empirically supported and cu......... .... .ngenious system
that bring new life to the applicability of projective testing across
multiple clinical settings."

Anthony Castro, Ph.D., PsyD. *Department of Psychiatry,*
University of Miami Miller School of Medicine

A Cross-Cultural Psychological Assessment Manual

This user-friendly manual provides a cross-cultural psychological assessment battery, including projective methods. Authors outline a new, empirically validated, reliable system, which seeks to update the scoreable and interpretable factors and entwine commonly respected "tried and true" graphomotor tests, thereby maximizing their efficacy in the assessment of significant psychological traits in children and adults.

Because of its use as a gender fair, culture free, language free testing method, it will be a valuable asset in all areas of current psychological assessment. The CCPAB test takes approximately 20 to 40 minutes to administer, and does not require any administration materials that most practitioners would not have readily available. The CCPAB can be used by evaluators on its own or in conjunction with other psychological and neuropsychological test data, as well as by mental health treatment providers seeking a quick and accurate way to assess the psychological functioning of individuals aged six years and older. Multiple appendices contain information on scoring criteria, scoring keys, and a wealth of sample questions which will also be a useful resource for evaluators.

This manual is appropriate for users ranging from graduate-level students in training and supervision to even the most skilled assessment psychologists for quick and valid assessment of a wide range of clients.

Alan J. Raphael, Ph.D., ABAP is Board Certified in Assessment Psychology. He is the CEO of International Assessment Systems, Inc. He is a former Adjunct Associate Professor of Psychology at the University of Miami. He is the co-developer of the Advanced Psychological and Neuropsychological Scoring System for the Bender Gestalt Test. Dr. Raphael is the President of the American Board of Assessment Psychology and a Fellow of the American Academy of Assessment Psychology. He is the former co-editor of the *Archives of Assessment Psychology* journal. He has published three books and over 30 professional articles.

Dr. R. Lauren Miller, Psy.D., J.D. is the Associate Clinical Director and a Consultant for International Assessment Systems, Inc., where she provides neuropsychological and psychological testing to personal injury litigants for issues related to brain injury, psychological trauma, and/ or vocational rehabilitation. Dr. Miller served as an adjunct faculty member and clinical supervisor for seven years, teaching and training doctoral-level assessment and psychopathology.

Theresa Ascheman Jones, Psy.D. is a Forensic Psychologist and conducts evaluations for the Court regarding competency to stand trial and violence risk. She is the primary neuropsychological evaluator and consultant at a forensic hospital. She regularly serves as an expert witness to the Court.

Charles J. Golden, Ph.D., ABAP, ABCN, ABPN is internationally known for his clinical research in neuropsychological assessment. He has given over 1000 presentations, posters, and workshops, and published over 500 articles, book chapters, and books. He is a Fellow of the American Psychological Association, and holds a Diplomate in Clinical Psychology, Clinical Neuropsychology, and Psychological Assessment. He received the *Distinguished Neuropsychologist Award* from the National Association of Neuropsychologists in 2003.

A Cross-Cultural Psychological Assessment Manual
The Raphael Methodology

Alan J. Raphael, R. Lauren Miller,
Theresa Ascheman Jones, and
Charles J. Golden

Routledge
Taylor & Francis Group

NEW YORK AND LONDON

Designed cover image: © Getty Images

First published 2024
by Routledge
605 Third Avenue, New York, NY 10158

and by Routledge
4 Park Square, Milton Park, Abingdon, Oxon, OX14 4RN

*Routledge is an imprint of the Taylor & Francis Group, an
informa business*

ISBN: 978-1-032-31252-1 (hbk)
ISBN: 978-1-032-31253-8 (pbk)
ISBN: 978-1-003-30879-9 (ebk)

DOI: 10.4324/9781003308799

Typeset in Sabon
by MPS Limited, Dehradun

Contents

Acknowledgements

The authors wish to thank Monica Gamez, M.S., Chantel Sorochuck, M.S., Scott Harcourt, M.S., Hilary Hayhurst, M.S., and Jacqueline Marsh, M.S. for serving as raters in the inter-rater reliability study. Additionally, the authors thank Monica Gamez, M.S. for assisting in providing resources for the literature review and aiding in research logistics and Chantel Sorochuk, M.S. for extensive data entry.

Foreword

This well-written, concise test manual brings a new, empirically validated, reliable system to psychological assessment practitioners and graduate students in many areas of psychology and in most cultures. The current system (CCPAM) combines and updates the scorable and interpretable factors of the time honored and well-respected House Tree Person, Draw A Person, Bender Gestalt, Kinetic Family Drawing and Free Drawing tests. I believe that this publication will find widespread use throughout the psychological and mental health communities as well as in the National Association of School Psychologists (NASP), the Society for Personality Assessment and the American Psychological Association (APA) as well and many international organizations involved in psychological testing of adults and children.

The CCPAM is the only system of its kind that seeks to integrate and update the scorable and interpretable factors of these time-honored tests, thereby increasing the power of the methods by bundling them and including evidence-based research. This manual's inclusion of objective scoring criteria makes it an especially valuable tool not only in clinical practice but also in research design, as it allows for easy replication and expansion of studies.

The empirical research for this system began in the late 1980s by an independent team of researchers with the first test manual published in 1992 and is continuing to the present day across multiple sites and studies. The format of the CCPAM is patterned in the style of other widely used test batteries such as the Halstead-Reitan Neuropsychological Battery (HRNB) and Luria-Nebraska Neuropsychological Battery (LNNP), the latter of which was developed by one of the co-authors of the CCPAM, Dr. Charles Golden. The CCPAM provides a brief, culture fair, gender fair battery of personality assessment with some relevance to neuropsychological assessment. It takes approximately 20 to 40 minutes to administer, and does not require any administration materials other than unlined white paper and sharpened #2 pencil. The authors caution that the CCPAM should be used by evaluators in conjunction with other psychological and neuropsychological test data. It is also useful to mental health treatment providers seeking a quick and more accurate way to assess the psychological functioning of individuals ages six years and older.

The manual includes easy-to-follow administration, scoring, and interpretive guidelines for the system. It also includes numerous illustrations of actual test protocols and case examples demonstrating the utility of the system within a complete psychological evaluation. A review of the literature and research relevant to projective psychological assessment is included. Comparison and contrast between previously devised methods of interpreting projective drawing tests and the CCPAB will be discussed.

Historically, projective tests including the Rorschach, TAT and projective drawing tests are frequently used in psychological evaluations globally, providing rich diagnostic clinical data in formulation of treatment recommendations and treatment outcomes.

The tests included are recognized globally as language-free, culture-fair, and gender-fair measures that do not require reading skills and can be rapidly administered and scored. Also, these measures are less susceptible to motivational factors. While these tests have been more frequently used to evaluate children, the data analyses conducted to examine results of the CCPAM includes data for children, adolescents, and adults, and this data will increase evidence for the utility of these measures across the lifespan.

This manual should be especially helpful for members of the Society for Personality Assessment who utilize projective measures as well as for other psychologists who use paper and pencil tests to evaluate personality.

In sum, although clinical practitioners involved in the use of psychological assessment remain highly likely to benefit from this manual; however, researchers and their assistants, teachers and their students, as well as supervisors and trainees, also are included among the interest consumers of this methodology. This manual has diagnostic value in Personality Assessment, Psychological Testing, Projective Testing, Clinical Psychology, Pediatric Psychology, School Psychology, Neuropsychology, Geropsychology, Rehabilitation Psychology, Counseling Psychology and Licensed Mental Health Practitioners involved in Assessment activities.

Norman Abeles, Ph.D., ABAP
Past president of the American Psychological Association;
Professor Emeritus of Psychology, Michigan State University;
and Board Certified in Assessment Psychology

Preface

This test manual brings a new, empirically validated, reliable system into the armamentarium of psychometrically minded clinicians. *A Cross-Cultural Psychological Assessment Manual: The Raphael Methodology* (CCPAM) seeks to update the scoreable and interpretable factors and entwine commonly respected "tried and true" graphomotor tests, thereby maximizing their efficacy in the assessment of significant psychological traits in children and adults. Because of its use as a gender fair, culture free, language free testing method, it will be a valuable asset in all areas of current psychological assessment.

Furthermore, unlike older publications that only focus on single assessment methods with little research and consensus regarding interpretation, the CCPAM includes a collection of assessment techniques with more recent research and empirically validated scoring criteria. Its empirical basis has been in development for over 30 years of studies that started in the late 1980s by an independent team of researchers at the University of Miami and has continued to present day across multiple sites and studies. It also incorporates research from other well-validated personality assessment methods such as the Bender Gestalt Test (BGT).

Context

In the long history of psychological testing research and clinical practice, many psychologists viewed delineating details on any objective, projective assessment measure as a sophisticated method of assessing traits that are difficult to manipulate, conceal, or modify. Proponents of projective testing, particularly graphomotor testing, viewed any oddity of inclusion or omission and any distortion be considered for objective scoring or interpretation by the examiner. Previously, it had been difficult to describe each specific response obtained and its corresponding interpretation. Variables such as age, ethnicity, gender, physical status, education, and reason for evaluation must be considered in the accurate scoring and interpretation of all psychological measures.

Theoretical underpinnings for the CCPAM stem from psychoanalytic thinkers and clinicians going back to the early 20th century. Freud, Jung, Fenichel, Bender, Rorschach, Binswanger, and others built the foundation on which the current system stands. Ongoing developments from psychometricians like Hutt, Weiner, Exner, Dahlstrom, and Bortner helped create measures that could be empirically validated. Ongoing research responding to psychometric criticisms of projective methods has continued into the 21st century. The persistence of such efforts is reflective of the enduring interest across generations of practitioners through the present day to further the validity, research methodology, and clinical utility of such measures.

The CCPAM is the only system of its kind that seeks to integrate and update the scoreable and interpretable factors of these time-honored tests, thereby increasing the power of the methods by bundling them and including evidenced based research. This manual's inclusion of objective scoring criteria makes it an especially valuable tool not only in clinical practice but also in research design, as it allows for easy replication and expansion of studies. The emphasis of such duplicable research criteria has been emphasized in recent studies (Smith, Gacono, Fontan, Cunliffe & Andronikof, 2020) as imperative to furthering the integrity of projective assessment research and preserving the psychometric properties of such measures, including inter-rater reliability, internal validity, and external validity. These properties bear directly on the clinical utility of the assessment methods, informing issues ranging from test selection to interpretation. This manual is designed to guide the user through such issues in an intuitive and user-friendly format. This structure, incorporating standardized administration and objective scoring criteria, facilitates ease of training and application in a consistent and reliable manner. Its inclusion of case examples is particularly illustrative of the "real world" application and usefulness of the manual's methods.

In sum, clinical practitioners involved in the use of psychological assessment remain highly likely to benefit from this manual. Researchers and their assistants, teachers and their students, as well as supervisors and their trainees, also are included among the interest consumers of this methodology.

Format

The format of the CCPAM is patterned in the style of other test batteries such as the Halstead-Reitan Neuropsychological Battery (HRNB) and Luria-Nebraska Neuropsychological Battery (LNNB), the latter of which was developed by one of the co-authors of the CCPAM, Dr. Charles Golden. Unlike these batteries of neuropsychological functioning, however, the CCPAM provides a brief battery of personality assessment. It takes approximately 20 to 40 minutes to administer, and it does not require any administration materials that most practitioners would not have handy, namely paper and pencil.

CCPAM can be used by evaluators on its own or in conjunction with other psychological and neuropsychological test data, as well as by mental health treatment providers seeking a quick and accurate way to assess the psychological functioning of individuals ages six years and older. Because of its relatively unstructured and unintrusive administration, it is a particular useful took for assessing subconscious aspects of personality that may not otherwise be revealed upon self-report.

Cross-Cultural Considerations

Furthermore, recent trends in clinical research and practice have increasingly focused on issues of cross-cultural applicability of assessment methods to diverse populations. Historical pitfalls in the usage of some personality tests with individuals of cultural backgrounds different from that of the test's normative sample(s) have regrettably raised issues of cultural fairness and social justice. For example, tests of intellectual functioning tend to underestimate the cognitive abilities of children of minority backgrounds and therefore result in their disproportionate exclusion from gifted education programs. While this manual's methods are not intended to assess intellectual functioning, they are intended to reduce such potentially discriminatory conclusions. Accordingly, administration techniques are less language-based and more nonverbal, thereby reducing bias in administration and interpretation and increasing reliability and validity of the results. This format is not only ideal for use with individuals of various ethnicities, but also for people within a broad range of ages and developmental abilities whose language comprehension skills might otherwise confound accurate personality assessment. These and other cultural considerations are expounded throughout the manual.

1 Introduction

Historically, psychologists and psychometricians in the United States first gained prominence during World War II when psychometric testing proved itself as a quick, cost-effective method of assessing individuals, alone or in groups, for the various branches of the Armed Forces. The unique aspect of psychological testing, as compared to psychiatric interviews, rested on the fact that psychological testing provided statistically significant, reliable information of which the individual being evaluated may not have been consciously aware or, more often, did not necessarily want to share with the psychologist for a variety of reasons.

Additionally, large numbers of individuals could be evaluated simultaneously using a battery of sophisticated psychological measures, while interviews were limited to one interviewee at a time. While the validity and reliability of any one test may have been roughly equivalent to that of any one interview, an organized, planned group or battery of psychological tests enhanced the accuracy of the clinical picture and increased the number of individuals who could be accurately assessed in a very brief period of time. Psychological test batteries also measured multiple traits, including personality, psychopathology, neurological status, intellectual capacity, motivation, and the issue of malingering far better and more efficiently than clinical interviews.

Assessment psychologists have always grappled with the fact that an examination using only one particular measure (i.e., test or interview) during psychological or neuropsychological assessments vastly increases the probability of error in interpretation. The likelihood of error is greatly reduced as the number of various measures increases, assuming they are reliably administered and scored. This is the major justification for utilizing a group or battery of measures, which can provide accurate confirmation or rejection of initial diagnostic impressions.

According to Rapaport et al. (1968), personality measures should be somewhat unstructured and have a degree of ambiguity. These criteria allow clinicians to derive information about personality without allowing that information to be influenced by the examinee's perception of social acceptability. Projective tests or techniques are so named

DOI: 10.4324/9781003308799-1

because the examinee projects his or her own ideations and perceptions onto the test. Rapaport and colleagues further described projective procedures as "… procedures in which the subject actively and sponta- neously structures unstructured material, and in so doing reveals his structuring principles – which are the principles of his psychological structure" (Rapaport et al., 1968). Hence, projective test findings are more difficult to manipulate consciously and the findings more accurate reflections of the true psychological make-up of the examinee.

The authors also emphasized the importance of quantitative scoring systems to produce objective results and cited the Thematic Apperception Test (TAT) as a measure that lacks a quantitative scoring system. Grapho- motor drawing tests yield new, additional and important facets of pro- jective test evaluation. Figure drawings include the House, Tree, Person, and Kinetic Family drawings. The Free drawing test is often administered in conjunction with the figure drawings, as is the Bender Gestalt geometric shape test. The use of drawings to evaluate nonverbal intelligence was pioneered by Florence Goodenough in 1926 with the creation of her "Draw-A-Man" Test, which has since been adapted to many variations. This procedure requires the examinee to draw a picture of a human male figure. Two subsequent variations are Machover's 1949 "Draw-A- Person" test (DAP), and Koppitz's 1968 "Emotional Indicators" for children based on human- figure drawings.

The History of Projective Drawing Tests

Projective drawing tests have had a prominent place in psychological assessment for almost 100 years. Goodenough's 1926 text is commonly recognized as the earliest use of drawing tests in psychological assessment; however, her work was limited to examining intellectual functioning and did not incorporate personality assessment. An extension of Goodenough's 1926 work, Buck's 1948a House-Tree-Person Test (H-T-P), was developed to assess both intelligence and personality functioning.

As part of her clinical expertise, Machover (1949) addressed person- ality assessment through human figure drawings, as she studied drawing qualities that appeared typical of various clinical groups. Though she reported impressive agreement in her interpretations of drawings with other measures, including the Rorschach, her work remained mostly at the case study phase, and more thorough empirical support was not achieved. Of her case study evaluations, the author noted, "It may, in the future, be necessary to develop some system of scoring for purposes of teaching, but for the present it has been found most fruitful to deal directly with the figure for interpretation" (Machover, 1949; p. 28).

Koppitz (1968) developed a system of interpretation for the human figure drawings of 5- to 12-year-old children. She described the system as both "projective," that is, measuring "unconscious needs, conflicts, and personality traits" and "a developmental test of mental maturity" (p. 1). Specifically, Koppitz reported that her system examined developmental stage and interpersonal attitudes and was based on Harry Stack Sullivan's Interpersonal Relationship Personality Theory. To address the developmental aspect of her system, Koppitz (1968) collected frequency data of 30 drawing features (e.g., head, facial features, body, etc.) and analyzed the occurrence of these features across age and gender groups. The features were then classified as being "Expected," "Common," "Not Unusual," or "Exceptional." Few of the items were found to relate to age and gender; however, "Expected" and "Exceptional" items were found to be useful in devising a screening measure of "mental maturity" (p. 34) as they were significantly correlated with WISC and Stanford-Binet IQ scores.

The projective portion of Koppitz's system included 38 items that were classified as "Quality signs," (e.g., broken or sketchy lines, transparencies), "Special features," (e.g., tiny head, crossed eyes), or "Omissions" (e.g., omission of eyes, omission of legs). Of the 38 items, 32 met the criteria set in a normative study, which required they were not related to age and maturation and were present in 15% or less of the drawings of children in specific age groups. In validation studies, 30 items were found to be valid emotional indicators that could differentiate between children in the clinical sample and the normal sample. Following her initial system development, Koppitz applied her emotional indicators to adolescents and asserted that the interpretations of the indicators were more useful when grouped into eight categories: Impulsivity; Insecurity, Feelings of Inadequacy; Anxiety; Shyness, Timidity; Anger, Aggressiveness (Koppitz, 1984). The method for developing these categories is somewhat unclear; however, the author did provide results of chi square analysis showing statistically significant differences in indicators of Impulsivity, Insecurity/Inadequacy, and Anger/Aggression between students with and without learning disability.

Despite their longevity and popularity, most projective drawing tests lack strong empirical support as measures of personality, indicators of trauma, or the host of psychological issues that they are used to assess. This has likely contributed to the lack of consensus on teaching, using, and interpreting projective drawing tests. Contemporary skepticism of the H-T-P is suggested by Groth-Marnat's (2003) recommendation to use the measure to assess visuo-constructive abilities, but only as a supplement to more researched measures, such as the Bender Gestalt Test. Several qualitative and quantitative scoring systems have been devised for the H-T-P and the DAP, though none have provided strong enough support to gain unanimous use or majority acceptance among clinicians. Gillespie (1994) promoted validation by advising examiners to compare results of Mother-and-Child drawings with MMPI profiles; however, the author did not provide empirical analysis of statistical relationship between the drawing test and the objective MMPI, which could have provided more support for the validity of drawing tests. Furthermore, this type of research was precluded by an absence of well-defined scoring guidelines in Gillespie's manual, in which the author advises an individualized approach to interpretation. While considering each individual examinee in interpreting results and never interpreting drawings in isolation of other measures are good clinical practices, they do not promote empirical evidence for use of specific scoring systems.

Some systems have integrated the H-T-P with the DAP, in that inquiries from the DAP are used to gather information about the person drawings of the H-T-P. The H-T-P is commonly followed by a "Free Drawing," in which the examinee is asked to draw anything of his or her choice, apart from a house, a tree, or a person. Family drawing, including the Kinetic-Family-Drawing Test, is another commonly used evaluation measure, which provides information about self-perception and interpersonal relationships, particularly those of the family of origin.

There are ever-increasing demands placed on the social sciences to create more efficient, more accurate and less expensive methods of assessing the validity of test results and outcomes, such as fitness for duty, competence, dangerousness, self-control, and many others. Despite the hesitation regarding the validity and reliability of projective tests, a time-honored theme in personality research is the axiom that an individual's productions, be they verbal, written, or otherwise, accurately define that person's inner or covert perceptions. As early as 1912, in Austria, Sigmund Freud recognized that one's expression of internal processes was central to the understanding of that person's psychology. Freud (1912-1913), in discussing projection, explained:

> "The projection of inner perception to the outside world is a primitive mechanism, which, for instance, also influences our sense perceptions, so that it normally has the greatest share in shaping our outer world (p. 107–108)."

Regardless of the specialty of the examiner (e.g., Forensic, Clinical, Counseling, Educational or Neuropsychological), a strong background in personality theory is essential when using projective drawing measures. If one does not have a solid understanding of human behavior upon which to draw psycho-diagnostic impressions, his or her interpretive accuracy will likely suffer. For example, the present authors received a neuropsychological evaluation that boldly proclaimed that "no anxiety was present" in the individual being evaluated, only to conclude that the person's diagnosis was a "generalized anxiety disorder." As psychology becomes more specialized, there exists an increasing danger of piecemeal and errant understanding of human behavior in general and psycho-diagnosis and treatment recommendations in particular.

Diversity Considerations

Intra-individual variables must be considered in the scoring and interpretation of any projective or objective measure. The same type of response may have a completely different meaning for a child, a geriatric patient, or a young adult. For example, a psychologist with limitations in training might take a patient's Rorschach response and search through various Rorschach reference books until he or she comes across the particular response given, then search for another response and find it in yet another book by a different author with a different approach and use that interpretation for that response. Such actions do not take into account the dynamics of each individual and, sadly, reflect both the myopic and compulsive dynamics of the tester more than any other factor. This method also poses a risk of over-pathologizing the examinee. Repeated indications of severe pathology on multiple measures are necessary to formulate a diagnosis of some type of major psychological illness.

There recently has been increased focus on intra-individual gender identity variables. Many commonly administered objective personality tools (e.g., self-report inventories and behavior rating scales) prompt the test-taker to identify the gender of the person being assessed within a dichotomous format, namely male or female. For individuals who do not identify with the historically traditional gender binary, presentation of such prompts may result in the test taker becoming confused, intimidated, and/or skeptical of the evaluator's competence and understanding of the participant's identity. This could be damaging for rapport, potentially impact the participant's engagement in the assessment and thereby affect the validity of the results.

In contrast, the CCPAM does not require a participant to identify their gender. Although some interpretive considerations are offered for drawing features depicted by a "male" or a "female," the clinician is advised to exercise clinical judgment in the context of understanding the participant's self-ascribed gender identity as well as other intra-individual variables. The authors acknowledge the spectrum of gender identity along which human experience ranges, and strictly warns against any of the CCPAM techniques being used to label, pathologize, discriminate, or otherwise alienate any person on the basis of gender identity.

It is unknown whether the CCPAM research sample contained any participant(s) who did (or do) not identify as "male" or "female." Drawings were collected across research sites from the early 1980s to the present day and unfortunately, data collection about gender identity has been limited to binary classification until recently. The authors encourage users and researchers of the CCPAM to continue to study the interaction of gender variables with use of the test battery.

Process Considerations

Process factors like tempo, erasures, and resistance are important in the overall analysis of paper and pencil drawing tests. Some psychological tests produce more resistance or anxiety than others. The drawing tests, like the Rorschach, often produce a situation wherein the subject is asked to complete an unclear task that he or she perceives may have "right or wrong" answers. Therefore, anxiety and resistance can immediately increase. Common resistance indicators that should be noted would include any spontaneous, extraneous verbalizations, interruptions to ask questions, humorous comments, or attempts to leave the office to use the restroom or get a drink of water. It is axiomatic that unsolicited verbal productions often point to anxiety, defensiveness, or intellectualization.

In contrast, the Sentence Completion, the Thematic Apperception Test (TAT), the MMPI-2, and most other language-based psychological tests provide a sense of assurance that the subject can successfully modify information through conscious control. Conscientious, rule-bound subjects are sensitive to looking "foolish" and may approach the drawings with apprehension and anxiety. Adults with these characteristics are known to make comments, such as "I can't draw" or "I'll draw what I did when I was a kid," when asked to draw a house or a person. It is for this reason that it is recommended that the examiner begin each psychological battery with a biographical data sheet (or Face-Sheet) and the Bender Gestalt Test (API System), which are more familiar and less threatening. Due to the relative simplicity of these measures, less resistance is likely to occur if the evaluation begins in this order. The remaining sequence of tests should be relatively unimportant and can be left to the discretion of the individual examiner.

Tempo and sequence of test performance provide often under-recognized but potentially important information for final interpretation of any of the psychological measures. Impulsivity must figure into the final analysis of rapidly completed measures as should the obvious obsessive-compulsive configuration of a patient who works more slowly than usual. There is a significant difference between the individual with mania who is extremely expansive and the constricted, compulsive individual who may be coping with covert paranoid ideation. The individual with mania or expansiveness will demonstrate the same general expansiveness throughout the test battery both in terms of responses as well as in behavior, while the constricted, compulsive person is likely to demonstrate the evasive, circumspect behavior consistently throughout the evaluation.

If a subject rapidly and uncritically completes most of the drawing tests and then works slowly and painstakingly on one specific drawing test, the importance of that particular measure to the overall information derived must be carefully considered. The same consideration applies for any test where the amount of time spent is significantly different than the time spent for the balance of the measures. This concept is comparable to the meaningful behavior in tempo and sequence that occurs in dealing with the Rorschach Inkblots or the Minnesota Multiphasic Personality Inventory-2 (MMPI-2) or the MMPI-2-RF. Consistency of responses is a major factor in the final compilation of clinical conclusions. For example, malingering or secondary gain behavior must be considered if expansive response patterns are combined with obsessive-compulsive restriction.

Additionally, if a projective measure involves a paper and a pencil, erasures are of extreme interpretive importance. Erasures usually occur when the subject feels the desire to improve the produced drawing. Improvement often involves anxiety and self-criticalness. The absence of erasures often implies a lack of self-criticalness potentially indicative of narcissistic and sociopathic traits. What is erased, where and how erasures occur, and whether any improvement occurs after the erasures are all significant and should always be considered in the final interpretation. Of course, it is the examiner's responsibility to provide the examinee with several sharpened pencils with adequate erasers. The absence of such essential materials could be interpreted as punitive or passive-aggressive behavior on the part of the examiner.

Erasures usually occur when the subject feels, for whatever reason, that they somehow did not do the drawing correctly and desire to improve it. The anxiety and self-criticalness generated by the particular design or drawing where the attempts at improvement occur must then be considered. Generally, "improvement" refers to a pencil response more acceptable to the subject. If the subsequent attempt or attempts to redraw a design does not improve the drawing, the meaning attached to the erased drawing becomes stronger and more certain. For example, when reproducing Design 3 (the arrowhead) of the BGT, an adult male erased his reproduction of this design three times before finally completing it as smaller and less pointed then both his original attempts and the actual stimulus figure. This behavior implies difficulty with adult male functioning. The interpretation of difficulty with adult male functioning was further verified when he completed the sentence stem "I wish ..." of the Sentence Completion Form with the response, "I WISH I were a child again."

One must evaluate obvious omissions (e.g., a doorknob in the House Drawing); what is included and emphasized (e.g., accentuated ears on a Human Figure Drawing), and the length of response time on any given test, oral or written (e.g., a House Drawing in 20 minutes). It is often the case that the likely interpretation will only become evident when the balance of the projective measures in a test battery are obtained.

For all of the aforementioned reasons, hard and fast rules of interpretation are not always correct. Symbolic representations should be used only to guide the process of interpretation and not to portray the final analysis. Thus, the following chapters broaden the examiner's awareness of psychological assessment techniques in general and the intrinsic value of projective/symbolic interpretations in particular.

2 Administration

Appropriate Participants

Projective drawing tests are appropriate for use with individuals ages six and older. While some authors have used the methods with children as young as age five years, others caution against using projective drawing techniques with children younger than age seven due to the visual-motor demands of the tasks. For the purposes of this manual, the authors were able to collect sufficient normative data for use with population between the ages of 6 and 80.

In addition to having achieved a minimal chronological age to provide rich projective drawings, users are also encouraged to consider the cognitive and motor abilities of an individual as it relates to the appropriate use of the test. For example, those with attentional or impulse control problems may have difficulty understanding or complying with task instructions, maintaining focus on the task, and completing it thoughtfully. Similarly, individuals with fine motor impairment may not produce interpretable results, depending on the extent of their impairment.

Administration Needs and Considerations

The ideal administration setting for projective drawings is characterized by privacy, adequate lighting, and minimal environmental distractions. Sufficient rapport with the examinee should be established. The examiner should sit across from the examinee at a comfortable social distance to administer the drawings. The examiner will need at least seven pieces of plain white letter-size (8.5 × 11 inch) paper and several sharpened #2 pencils with erasers. The paper should not be good rag paper, nor a translucent typewriter paper, but of a quality that shows erasures. This will allow an evaluation of possible trouble areas in terms of emotional pressures where the erasures occur in all of the paper and pencil measures (e.g., Face Sheet, Bender Gestalt Test, House-Tree-Person Test, Draw-A-Person Tests with Inquiries, the Free Drawing, the Kinesthetic Family Drawing, the Thematic Apperception Test, the Sentence Completion Form, etc.).

DOI: 10.4324/9781003308799-2

It is important that subjects understand that only one drawing test (e.g., Draw-A-Person) is permitted per page. These instructions are especially critical after the administration of the Bender wherein the subject has been instructed not to place one design per page. If this is not made clear, the subjects may automatically assume that there will be other drawings on the page, and particularly if they are right-handed, are likely to place extremely small houses in the left-hand corner of the page. It is wise to make it obvious to the examinee that enough paper is available so that separates test can be completed on separate pages.

The Drawings

When all seven drawing tests will be given, the order of administration is as follows:

1   BGT (vertical paper presentation)
2   House (horizontal paper presentation)
3   Tree (vertical paper presentation)
4   Person (vertical paper presentation)
5   Person of the opposite gender (vertical paper presentation)
6   Kinetic Family Drawing (horizontal paper orientation)
7   Free Drawing (horizontal paper orientation)

Note, when house and tree drawings will not be given, begin administration with BGT or Person drawing. Also note that drawings 6 and 7 can be administered independently of the preceding five. Regarding item 6, these authors wish to distinguish the Kinetic Family Drawing (KFD) from the Draw-A-Family (DAF) method. The methods differ in the specificity of their instructions. DAF directs the examinee to "draw a family," while the KFD instructions are more directive, as described.

Administration Procedures

Drawing Phase

Following BGT Administration[1], place a sharpened #2 pencil with an eraser and an 8.5 × 11-inch piece of plain white paper oriented in the proper direction (as above specified) for the prompt you are presenting. Say to the examinee, "I would like you to draw as good a house as you can." Handler (2014) encourages examiners to maintain as little structure as possible during the administration. If the examinee asks for further clarification, simply encourage, "It's up to you." Unobtrusively note any remarkable behavioral observations of the participant while she or he is drawing, such as resistance, emotional response, and verbalizations made while drawing.

If the participant is resistant to engage in the task, use clinical judgment in addressing the resistance. If he or she expresses concern regarding drawing ability, encourage, "Do the best you can." Provide reassurance that the drawing will not be evaluated for artistic quality, and that there is no right or wrong way to do it. If resistance persists, the examiner may attempt to elicit specific concerns about task engagement, address such, and/or offer the participant a break or to complete the task at another time if possible. It may be noteworthy if the participant is resistant to only certain drawings. For example, a person may complete all drawings up until the KFD, which could provoke resistance if family is a source of conflict, confusion, and/or stress.

If the examinee produces a stick figure for either the person drawings, he or she should be thanked for their effort and then given a new piece of paper and instructed, "This time, I would like you to draw a whole person, not a stick figure." To administer the next human figure to drawing to a child, note, "You drew a boy, now draw a girl," or vice versa. For adults, instruct, "Now I would like you to draw a person of the opposite sex."

To administer the KFD, instruct, "Now draw a picture of your family doing something." As noted above, these directions distinguish this task from the DAF, which asks the examinee only to draw a family and neither specifies inclusion of the self nor engagement in an activity. These authors do not recommend instructing the examinee to include himself or herself, as the omission of the self from the family drawing, which sometimes occurs, can provide data about the perception of self in relation to other family members and the environment. Furthermore, instructing the examinee to show the family doing something may reveal richer information about family dynamics and the roles of each member.

Inquiry Phase (Optional)

Once the participant has completed all drawings to be administered, the examiner may elect to proceed with an inquiry phase. Although the scoring criteria are objective, the examiner may wish to collect additional qualitative information about the drawings. Such data may enhance the clinical utility of the objective scoring criteria by providing context for scorable features. This is a similar process to inquiring about critical items on self-report personality inventories; no one item is sufficient for interpretation but may provide nuance to more finely tune objective interpretation.

To begin the inquiry, each of the two Person drawings produced by the participant should be re-presented to him or her in the order in which they were administered. Upon presentation, the examiner prompts the examinee, "Tell me about this person." Note the response and ask follow up questions accordingly. For example, *What does this person like to do? What makes this person happy? What worries this person?*

What might happen to this person? Note the participant's responses to these questions for consideration of qualitative analysis. Users also may refer to

> It also may be appropriate to inquire about obviously remarkable visual features of the drawing such as disproportionately emphasized features, use of very heavy or very light markings, or omission of expected features. For example, *It looks as though this person does not have a mouth, please tell me more about that.* Again, note the participant's responses and reference them as needed during scoring and interpretation.

For the KFD, examiners should ask the examinee to identify each person and describe what is happening in the picture. Examiners should record verbatim the responses and ask follow-up questions for clarification as needed. For example, inquiring about the figure's identity, needs, thoughts, feelings, and expectations for the future may provide rich information about the examinee's inner world.

Scoring

See subsequent chapters for expanded scoring considerations. See Appendix A for a concise list of scoring criteria for HTP, KFD, and Free Drawing techniques.

Note

1 See Raphael, A. J., Golden, C., & Raphael, M. A. (2012). *The Advanced Scoring System for the Bender Gestalt Test- Revised (ABGT-R): Ages 8–80.* Deer Park, NY: Linus Publications, Inc.

3   House-Tree-Person Test

The House-Tree-Person drawing test is a series of separate drawing tests that is a remarkable instrument for reflecting social interaction capabilities, self-concept assessment, nurture loss conflicts, and cognitive or ideational turmoil in proportions that range from situational, environmental pressures (e.g., poor school test grades) to serious ideational disturbances (e.g., psychosis). In addition, each individual drawing, as with any measure that is less vulnerable to conscious manipulations, also gives direction as to what to look for or verify throughout the remainder of the psychological test battery. The subject's degree of attentiveness from one part of the projective test to the other or from one test to another, the change in terms of details, pencil strokes and, of course, any omissions or elaborations, are all of potential major interpretive significance. In addition, the placement on the page, the size of the drawing, and the personalization, if any, that occur contribute to the overall personality profile obtained from the psychological response patterns.

According to Buck (1948a), the H-T-P was "designed to aid the clinician in obtaining information concerning the sensitivity, maturity, and integration of a subject's personality, and the interaction of that personality with its environment (both specific and general)." (p. 151). The procedure included a drawing phase and an inquiry phase with structured questions. The CCPAM uses administration that is quite similar to Buck's (1948a) method, which directed clinicians to request that examinees draw as good a house, tree, and person as possible while allowing unlimited time and use of erasure. Buck (1948a) advised to instruct examinees before they begin to draw full people rather than just a head and shoulders, while the CCPAM provides less structure in order to glean potential behavioral scores. While it is advisable to take adequate behavioral observation notes, the CCPAM does not follow Buck's (1948a) method of documenting the exact order in which each detail is drawn. Buck's (1948a, 1948b) system included quantitative and qualitative scoring; however, critics have expressed doubt about the validity and reliability of research methods (Killian, 1984), including those used in the revised manual (Buck, 1981). Buck (1948a) asserted that H-T-P

DOI: 10.4324/9781003308799-3

drawings correlated with IQ scores derived from the Stanford-Binet and the Wechsler-Bellvue. An inadequate sample size, lack of random stratified sampling, unclear inclusion criteria, and unreported demographics of subjects have been cited as methodological flaws in the development of Buck's (1948a) system (Killian, 1984).

One of very few recent empirically studied scoring systems, Van Hutton's (1994) H-T-P and DAP scoring system, was designed to gather information on personality and emotional characteristics of children with a history of sexual abuse. The 90 scoring items were drawn from a review of the literature and categorized into four subscales, which include Preoccupation with Sexually Relevant Concepts; Aggression and Hostility; Withdrawal and Guarded Accessibility; and Alertness for Danger, Suspiciousness, and Lack of Trust. Each subscale includes an item related to behavioral observations of the examinee. In addition to scoring the presence of each score item, administrators are to note their degree of certainty in the rating as low, medium, or high. The author tested the inter-rater reliability of the system by comparing consistency between two clinicians' scoring of the drawings of 20 children. After revisions of several items, the raters were in agreement 93.2% of the time, and each scoring item met the cutoff criteria of being consistently rated 80% of the time on the drawings of 10 additional child subjects. The control sample included 145 children age seven to twelve, excluding children with a history of diagnosed psychosis, developmental disability, or neurological impairment. Interpretive ranges of percentile scores were derived using the Johnson-curve method. Two independent raters scored 41 drawings of children in the clinical and control samples, and correlation coefficient for the four subscales ranged from .97 to .70. To evaluate the validity of the scoring system as a screening measure of possible child sexual abuse, H-T-P and DAP drawings from 20 sexually abused children, 20 emotionally disturbed but non-abused children, and 145 controls were scored. On the Sexually Relevant Concepts subscale, sexually abused children scored the highest followed by emotionally disturbed but non-abused children, followed by controls. Sexually abused males scored higher than other groups on the Aggression and Hostility subscale. On the Withdrawal and Guarded Accessibility subscale, sexually abused and emotionally disturbed but non-abused children scored higher than controls, and there was no main effect for gender. The Alertness for Danger, Suspiciousness, and Lack of Trust subscale was designated as a research scale as no significant group differences were found. The authors also examined the raw score frequency distributions of the samples to establish cutoff scores for the most accurate classification. The Sexually Relevant Concepts subscale correctly classified 97% of males and 98% of females. The Aggression and Hostility subscale correctly classified 96% of males and 85% of females. The Withdrawal and Guarded Accessibility subscale correctly classified

90% of children. Notably, the system was not examined in its ability to discriminate between sexual abuse and non-sexual physical abuse, and the authors listed this as an issue for future research.

In 2014, Handler reported that there is less research on house drawings than there is on other figure drawings. Buck and Handler have proposed a set of post-drawing inquiries to be asked of the examinee regarding the house drawing. Interpretation has traditionally been offered from a Kohution point of view (Handler, 2014). Other users have theorized the house drawing to represent either or both a) aspects of the self and b) a potential setting for family interactions.

House Drawing Test Interpretations

House Dimensions

The house drawing, regardless of the age of the subject, reflects interpersonal relationships, maturation, or movement toward adulthood as seen in the final realization of a three-dimensional house in a mature adult. Anything less than a three-dimensional house from an adult, particularly an individual with high-level schooling, represents regression, resistance, and guardedness in exposing personal conflicts or disturbed ideation in interpersonal relationships. The resistance that occurs in drawing a one-dimensional, simple "face" house (i.e., a rectangular box (face), two windows (eyes), a door (mouth), and a triangular roof (hair)) by a college graduate often is seen in combination with a guarded Rorschach Inkblot protocol in which the examinee provides ten or fewer responses. When this circumspect behavior is seen consistently throughout most or all of the test battery, it suggests the strong likelihood of difficulty relating to people and dealing with anxiety-producing material in therapy. These individuals usually are amenable to brief, symptom-focused treatment or treatment where the focus is shared with another person (e.g., marital or family therapy). They are poor candidates for therapies requiring exploration of feelings. Alternatively, the drawing of a two-dimensional "face" house can be an indication of severely limited intellectual abilities.

Two-dimensional homes, regardless of the age of the subject, drawn with windows reflecting multiple stories should be interpreted as pseudo striving and indicative of the limited ability of the individual to sustain goal directed behavior. If the subject is a married or cohabiting adult, it also suggests that the subject's spouse or partner is called upon to be the successful and responsible one.

Humanization

The academically advanced subject may be uncritical when reproducing the Bender but becomes resistant with a more intimidating projective measure like the House-Tree-Person Test. For example, a hospitalized 32-year-old female collage graduate diagnosed with schizophrenia who drew a simple two-dimensional face house paused after completing the drawing, then stated, "Oh, I forgot the eyes," and placed a dot in the center of each of the two windows. This humanization of an inanimate object reflects severe psychopathology similar to a contaminated percept in a Rorschach Inkblot protocol.

House Placement

Once the subject understands the directions, the placement of the house on the page is important. Young children very often place the house at the bottom edge of the page, emphasizing their security needs and resulting anxiety, since the bottom of the page is seen as a "security line" or foundation, similar to the side edge of the paper in drawing the Bender. Adults who use the bottom edge of the paper as the foundation in their house drawings would be extremely anxious, insecure, and immature individuals.

At times, subjects draw houses that do not fit on the page, with a portion of the house drawn off the page. These drawings raise questions concerning which areas or what rooms have been cut off or omitted. Most often, the bedroom has been excluded and points to the subject's sexual disturbances. Omitted kitchens point to dependency features while omitted living rooms point to peer relationship conflicts. Rooms that seem inaccessible should be interpreted as exaggerated disturbances in terms of whatever that room symbolically represents.

Unusual Perspectives

Aerial-view houses are houses drawn in three-dimensions that appear as though one is looking down from a height onto the house. These aerial-view houses most often are drawn by individuals of any age who tend to be extremely cautious and mistrustful in interpersonal relationships. They are also drawn by individuals with the role identification disturbances. These individuals use the "distance" to symbolize their real discomfort in close intimate relations. Typical of individuals with psychosis, paranoia, or profound gender dysphoria or gender identity disturbances, poor self-concepts hidden by detachment and isolation are suggested.

Similarly, floor plan houses are those that appear as a schematic of a house with no walls or roof. These types of house drawings to indicate even more severe pathology than aerial-view houses in terms of social isolation, paranoia and psychosis. While aerial-view houses represent detachment and a poor self-concept, floor-plan houses emphasize these traits to an even greater degree of turmoil. Individuals with regressive depression, paranoid schizophrenia, and schizoaffective disorder draw floor plan houses. Of course, the diagnosis of severe pathology must be confirmed with other test results.

House Shapes and Sizes

When young children take the H-T-P Drawing Test, their houses usually tend to be tall and narrow. The tall, narrow house reflects the limited social areas open to the young child. The limited social experiences also appear in the Tree and Human Figure Drawings and will be discussed in the sections of this text.

With both children and adults, house drawings can range from log cabins to igloos and often depend on where the subject resides or has previously resided. For example, igloos occur more frequently in the northwestern United States and Alaska should be questioned and interpreted if drawn by someone who has never lived in a cold climate. An igloo house was only seen once in 20,000 evaluations spanning 30 years by these examiners and was drawn by a frigid, obsessive-compulsive, super-ego driven woman who had lived her entire life in the southeast and had never seen an igloo in person. In this case, the balance of the protocol supported the conclusion that the igloo represented the cold, nurture-deficient upbringing experienced by this 41-year-old woman.

Tree houses are rarely drawn by adolescents and adults. When drawn by persons older than 12, they reflect immaturity, isolation, peer-relationship disturbances, eccentricity, and a desire to return to a younger, less responsible time in the life of the subject. The older the subject, the greater the likelihood of regressive functioning.

Houses that take up the majority of the page are typical of children and immature or neurologically impaired adolescents and adults. This expansiveness, when seen in neurologically intact individuals, usually reflects narcissistic, immature, anti-social functioning.

Roofs and Rooflines

When dealing with the overall structure of the house drawing test for children over the age of six, there should always be a definite dividing line between the roof (or attic) area and the living area of the house. Failure to include this dividing line raises questions regarding reality/ fantasy disturbances (e.g., schizophrenia). The absence of the dividing line in houses drawn by adolescents and adults is usually reflective of ideational turmoil and inadequate internal separation between fantasy (attic area) and reality (living area). Of course, this interpretation should be reconfirmed with other measures before concluding that severe psychopathology exists.

Individuals of all ages may draw a roof tiling or dividing lines in the roof area. When the dividing lines drawn in the attic/roof area are horizontal, the examinee can be said to be experiencing pressures from eco-syntonic ideation. Conversely, when the dividing lines are drawn vertically in the roof/attic area, the examinee is likely to be experiencing ego-dystonic, unacceptable ideation that often involves sexual turmoil. These individuals would be consciously involved in guarding or suppressing these unacceptable thoughts and behavior related to the overt expression of these thoughts (i.e., sexual perversion behavior).

A subject who begins to meticulously place tiles in the roof area of their house drawing but loses patience and finishes the roof area with scrolled lines, attempts to be obsessive-compulsive and apparently fails. The interpretation of giving up on tasks as a pattern of behavior would be consistent with this test behavior. On the other hand, carefully delineating tiles completely throughout the roof area as usually seen in a three-dimensional house suggests that the obsessive-compulsive defenses are operating excessively, and interpretations regarding functioning can be made for this individual.

The roof overhangs that protrude out past wall lines reflect paranoid ideation, even in young children. If the projections extend beyond or over the house wall lines due to elaborations, the possibility of the pressures of external forces on the personality should be considered. If any excessive or unusual introductions are made, they would be interpreted in terms of the dynamics dealing with unconscious pressures.

Roof Penetrations

On rare occasions, the roof/attic area lines are penetrated by other productions like a tree branch, the rays of the sun, or cloud drawings. These penetrations suggest disruptions or disturbances in the person's interpersonal experiences in general. Specifically, these intrusions usually suggest physical or sexual behavior that was traumatic for the examinee.

For example, a 13-year-old girl drew an elaborate three-dimensional house with an enormous sun radiating long rays through the roof area. In this particular case, the clinical material confirmed the long-term incestuous involvement with the adolescent's father. The excessive and unusual emphasis of the sun's rays penetrating through the roof area underscored the dynamics resulting from guilt, anxiety, and affective turmoil in this young girl.

Chimneys

Chimneys drawn on houses are important indicators of the impulse control capabilities in children and adults. Very young children (six and under) tend to draw chimneys that are tilted greater than or equal to 45 degrees from the roofline. As children move to adolescence, they begin to draw chimneys upright as would be expected. This modification in direction is based on the covert onset of puberty and the psycho-sexual and psycho-social factors found therein. In the authors' experience, the tilted chimney reflects the changes in psycho-sexual ideation in particular and social development in general. If these same children are retested at a more chronologically mature age (i.e., 12), it will be found that the chimney has assumed an upright position, suggesting the maturation in social functioning. Conversely, slanted chimneys drawn by adolescents or adult usually point to arrested, regressive, immature social functioning.

Chimneys drawn with smoke emerging indicate the degree of control or impulsivity demonstrated by the examinee, with more smoke indicating a greater degree of impulsivity. Care should be taken to note the intensity of the line quality and the degree of separation of the smoke from the chimney, which reflects denied acting-out behavior. Also, the darker the line quality of the smoke, the more impulsive the expression of anger would be.

The number of chimneys on the roof or the placement of the chimney over a particular room indicates the degree of conscious concern inherent in an individual related to impulse control. More than one chimney would suggest intense anxiety over loss of control and a psychotic preoccupation with control of unacceptable impulse. The placement of chimneys over a particular room can indicate the nature of the impulse with which the individual is concerned (e.g., a chimney over a bedroom may indicate concern related to sexual impulses).

Doors

Whether drawn by children or adults, houses usually include a front door. In evaluating the door treatment, the presence or absence of a doorknob is an important indicator of the individual's accessibility to relationships in general and specifically in therapy. The larger the doorknob in relation to the size of the door, the more accessible to treatment the person is likely to be. Absence of a doorknob suggests resistance to self-exploration and limited insight and, as such, is a clear indication that therapy is seen in threatening terms. Given the realities of health care economics, persons who are not accessible to treatment are less likely to benefit from it. The absence of the door itself is rare and would be seen as even more of a resistance indicator than just the failure to include a doorknob or latch. Other indications of being inaccessible include a flight of steps leading to the front door, markings in front of the door, a path leading up to but not quite meeting the lines of the door, or patio stones in front of the doorway, all of which suggest excessive resistance to cooperating in self-disclosure.

The placement of a second, additional door at the side of a house usually results from ambivalence and anxiety regarding the undertaking of counseling or treatment. While the accessibility symbols may be present on the front door, the likelihood of escape or avoidance through the side door must be considered. With these individuals, treatment is likely to be brief and, therefore, symptom reduction will likely precipitate a premature "flight into health," terminating counseling. Of course, these individuals reappear for treatment on an episodic or "crisis" basis and rarely make any substantial progress in resolving their difficulties. For these individuals, brief, symptom-focused treatment is the most productive.

For either gender, doors with a rounded top portion (e.g., phallic shaped) suggest the possibility of constant ideational pressure resulting from libid-inal pressures. On rare occasions, subjects have drawn some phallic shaped object (e.g., a tree) inside the door outline, which would be interpreted in terms of penetration trauma related to sexual trauma or sexual abuse.

Walls

A house that is drawn transparently has enormous clinical importance. The ability to see a staircase or people, for example, through the wall of the house (i.e., where there are no windows) should be perceived as an indication of serious ideational disturbance. In younger children, this may not be as pathological, but beyond the age of six, the question of primary process ideational turmoil (e.g., psychotic process) should be considered. Of course, as stated previously, repeated indications of severe pathology throughout an evaluation are necessary to formulate a diagnosis of psy-chosis, schizophrenia, or another type of severe mental illness.

Typically, in both two- and three-dimensional house drawings, the expected wall treatment consists of an unbroken line drawing. Whenever breaks occur in the wall line, consideration should be given to the pos-sibility of intermittent or episodic breaks in reality testing.

Windows

If our eyes are "windows to the soul," windows in a house drawing would be interpreted as the opportunities for being observed by others. Windows that are drawn near the roofline raise questions regarding fear of anyone "seeing inside," which usually ties in with severe emotional disturbance indicators (e.g., paranoia), seen on the other measures. The more seriously disturbed, paranoid individuals tend to place the windows touching or almost touching the roofline. If there is no roofline and the windows ex-tend up into the attic area, the pathology becomes even more definite.

Conversely, an enormous picture window placed close to the ground level raises questions regarding the exhibitionistic tendencies of the individual, which would be reflected in other measures as well as in their overall social interactions. Vertical lines on the windows (e.g., bars, vertical blinds) are most often drawn by adults, reflecting the likelihood of extreme caution regarding their ability to trust anyone.

Criss-crossed or cross-hatching lines in the window, including diagonal lines or a single vertical and single horizontal windowpane line, would reflect the tenuous ability or inability to maintain controls. If the cross-hatching or windowpane lines happen to extend through or beyond the window's outline, the lack of self-criticalness (e.g., lack of guilt) and the corresponding impulsivity are likely. Windowpane lines that strongly resemble a crucifix (e.g., the horizontal line crosses above the center point of the vertical line) suggest severe psychopathology, particularly when other indications of major mental illness are noted throughout the protocol. Such "crucifix" windows are drawn by individuals with schizophrenia or individuals with paranoid traits more often than by those in other clinical groups. The use of a "crucifix" symbol in drawing tests is a significant indicator for severe pathology, even if it is used appropriately, as on top of a Christmas Tree in a variation of a "Tree" Drawing test or on top of a church in a variation of a "House" drawing test. Of course, the less appropriate the crucifix symbol as to the drawing (e.g., as eye pupils), the greater the likelihood of the presence of psychopathology. The degree of religiosity in the individual does not minimize or diminish the pathological interpretation. Of course, religiosity per se is usually a protective factor in an individual of any age, but the pressure to introduce religious symbolism in this drawing test has clinical significance.

Rooms and Furniture

While it is rare for adults, often a young child will draw furniture in the various rooms and thusly indicate their high level of preoccupation or concern for a particular room. The corresponding interpretation should be consistent throughout the battery and would depend on what furniture is included and where, and conversely, on what furniture has been omitted. For example, including a dining room table but no chairs points to the possibility of nurture difficulties. A bedroom with no bed or a bathroom with no means of entrance or exit often indicates sexual concerns.

House Additions

When the instructions have been clearly specified with respect to only drawing a house and the subject includes additional features (e.g., a fence running on each side of the house, a mailbox in front of the house, birds, clouds, trees or the sun), these additions require the interpretation on ongoing ideation. Fences of all types usually signify guardedness, mistrust, paranoia, and poor social skills. If the fence is spiked, the additional interpretation of aggressivity should be included. A mailbox in front of the house, for either male or female subjects, raises questions regarding identity concerns (i.e., who lives here?). A drainpipe on the house raises questions about enuresis, particularly when it is dripping water.

Clouds usually represent a depressive mood regarding interpersonal functioning and dissatisfaction with self, and the greater the emphasis on the clouds, the deeper the depression. Birds in the sky, with or without clouds, also suggest depressive features of the personality structure. Similarly, kites and balloons are also indicators of dysphoria but may also point to external pressures and insecurity. Individuals who draw kites or balloons are more likely to be concealing their dysphoria (i.e., as would a "smiling depressive").

The sun symbolizes unresolved attachments to father. Including a moon in a house drawing is unusual, and celestial objects are more common, but still rare, in the Free Drawing test. They will be discussed in more detail in Chapter V. When included in the House Drawing test, the moon reflects a symbol of femininity in terms of the menstrual cycle, thus a moon drawing suggests ongoing conflicts with mother, particularly if the moon is half or less.

Landscapes are typically drawn by depressed and affectively isolated individuals, particularly when produced during the Free Drawing test; however, the interpretation of depressed affect is the same when there is a particular emphasis on landscape in the House Drawing test. A single ground line or horizon drawn with the House Drawing test should not be considered landscape. Interpretations of specific landscapes will be discussed in Chapter V.

Decorations such as flowers around the house usually occur with females, but not always. Excessive use of flowers or shrubs by females of all ages usually emphasizes the need to be seen as feminine and that feminine aspects are emphasized. Often, this type of addition suggests that the individual resorts to role-playing and manipulation in interpersonal relationships, particularly when the other person in the relationship is an older male. As usual, the greater the emphasis on the floral or shrubbery areas, the more likely the femininity is used as controlling behavior. Males who include flowers or shrubbery are likely to be struggling with their masculinity in conflicted and anxiety-producing ways. A classic example of the possible interpretation of a house drawing with flowers and shrubbery is that of Van Gogh's famous painting, "In Saint Remy and Auvers." In this timeless painting of a house, not only is the "fantasy line" missing between the roof and the balance of the house, but high shrubs and a wall along the road prevent anyone from seeing any entrance into the house. This would be interpreted as drawn by an adult with an inability to socialize. The striated markings along the top edge of the house near the chimney suggest repetitive disturbed ideation. There is no entrance to the house either through the shrub-lined road or through any other visible means, and the difficulty with reality and fantasy certainly would be consistent with what was said of a roofline separation in the drawing (Figures 3.1–3.47).

House Drawing Test Scores

1   Two dimensional houses:

Children (ages 17 and younger):
No interpretation
Adults (ages 18 and older):
Regression, resistance, and guardedness in exposing personal conflicts or disturbed ideation.

2   Face house, i.e., square or rectangular box (face), exactly two windows (eyes), door (mouth), and triangle roof (hair):

Children (ages 17 and younger):
No interpretation
Adults (ages 18 and older):
Resistance, circumspect behavior, or severely limited intellectual capabilities.

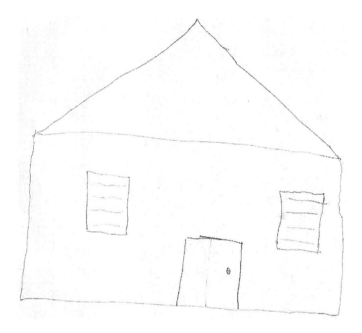

Figure 3.1 This "face house" was drawn by a 40-year-old woman who, despite involvement in psychotherapy, had not resolved her issues with self-dissatisfaction and the conflict between her role as a mother and housewife and her desire to work outside the home. Her house drawing did not indicate intellectual difficulties, as she functioned at an average or higher level intellectually and used intellectualization to resist the therapeutic relationship and to avoid dealing with emotional conflicts.

3   Windows reflecting multiple stories. The window(s) of the second story should be mostly above the horizontal mid-line to reflect multiple stories. This score would be applied when item #2 ("face house") is scored:

All ages:
Tendencies towards pseudo-striving and the limited ability of the individual to maintain goal-directed behavior. These individuals are often irresponsible, immature, and ineffectual and rely on the competence of their partners or families.

Figure 3.2 This house was drawn by an 8-year-old boy who had anxiety related to his parent's custody proceedings and particularly related to his mother's wellbeing following her surgical treatment for cancer. The boy reported no major subjective difficulties and appeared to put forth effort to be perceived as functioning well despite his covert anxiety.

4   Use of the bottom edge of the page as the base or foundation of the house:

Children and adolescents (ages 6 to 17):
Emphasizes developmental security deficits.
Adults (ages 18 and older):
Extreme anxiety and insecurity that reaches a pathological level.

5   A portion of the house does not fit on the page and is omitted:

All ages:
Interpretation requires inquiry regarding which rooms were cut off or omitted. Omitted kitchens point to dependency features; omitted bedrooms point to sexual concerns; omitted living rooms point to peer relationship conflicts.

Figure 3.3 This house, drawn by a 53-year-old female, uses most of the page and
trails off to the right side, suggesting that a portion of the house is not
visible and would continue off the page.

6   Aerial view houses:

All ages:
Extreme caution and mistrust in interpersonal relationships. Typical of individuals with psychosis, paranoia, or profound gender dysphoria or gender identification disturbances. Poor self-concepts hidden by detachment and isolation are suggested.

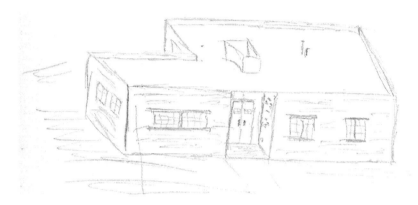

Figure 3.4 This aerial view house was drawn by a 46-year-old male who was seen in a correctional facility. He was experiencing intense stress related to the possible impact of his legal difficulties on his ability to maintain contact with his children.

7   Floor plan houses:

All ages:
Typical of severely isolated, paranoid, and psychotic teenagers and adults. The pathology is usually more severe with floor plan homes than with aerial view homes. Individuals with regressive depression, paranoid schizophrenia, and schizoaffective disorder draw floor plan houses.

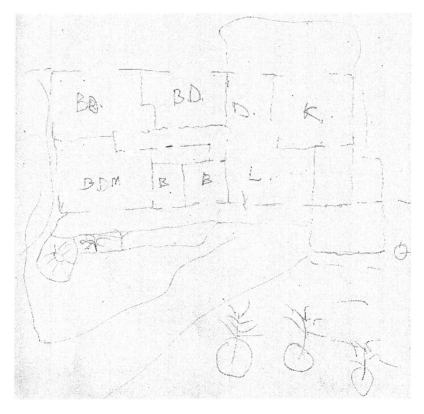

Figure 3.5 This floor plan drawing was produced by a 30-year-old man who had sustained a serious and life-altering physical injury. He demonstrated objective evidence of depression and exaggerated dependency on his MMPI, Rorschach, and Bender Gestalt Test profiles.

8   Transparent houses:

Ages 7 and younger:
No interpretation
Ages 8 and older:
Severe ideational turmoil. Primary process ideational turmoil (e.g., psychosis) should be considered.

Figure 3.6 This transparent house was drawn by a 42-year-old male with significant depression who believed his emotional difficulties to be due to a physical ailment despite a lack of evidence for any physical contribution.

9   Houses that take up 2/3 or more of the page in height, and are three inches or less in width, with emphasized chimneys (e.g., disproportionately larger or darkened, or attention to detail such as with brick work):

Ages 6 to 12:
Reflects the limited social areas open to the child.

Figure 3.7 This house was drawn by an 11-year-old boy whose parents were involved in a custody dispute of him and his younger sister. He lived with his mother, stepfather, sister, half-sister, and stepsister and had previously lived with his father. His mother was openly critical of him during the evaluation, and he had a history of anxiety and depressive symptoms as well as academic decline since residing with his mother.

Ages 13 and older:
No interpretation

10   Chimneys slanted ≥45° from vertical

Children (ages 12 and younger):
Normal. No interpretation
Ages 13 and older: Regression and immaturity in social functioning

Figure 3.8 This house was drawn by an intensely angry 18-year-old female who was a hospital inpatient. She demonstrated significantly regressed behavior in terms of impulsivity and acting out and was minimally cooperative with the evaluation, in part due to the belief that she had been "tricked" by her parents into being hospitalized.

11 Chimneys with smoke emerging:

All ages:
Important indicators of impulse control capabilities. Indicate impulsive expression of anger. The darker the line quality of the smoke, the more intense the anger and the weaker the controls on the expression of the anger.

Figure 3.9 This house was drawn by an 11-year-old boy with behavioral problems who attended a school for students with learning difficulties.

12 More than one chimney:

All ages:
Intense anxiety over loss of control and a psychotic preoccupation with control of unacceptable impulses. The greater the number of chimneys, the greater the degree of conscious concern related to impulse control.

13 Specific architectural style (e.g., log cabins, igloos, etc.):

All ages:
Reflects the individual's residence or prior residence. The scoring occurs if the individual has no experience in the type of house drawn. An igloo house is extremely rare and suggests frigid, obsessive-compulsive, and anhedonic traits. Tree houses are also very rare and reflect immaturity, isolation, eccentricity, peer disturbance and a desire to return to a less responsible time in the individual's life. The older the individual the greater the likelihood of regressive functioning.

14 Houses that take up more than 6 inches in width and 7 inches in height:

Children (ages 6–12):
No interpretation
Adolescents and adults (ages 13 and older):
Immaturity. This expansiveness also reflects neurological impairment. When the neurologic status is normal, the expansiveness is scored as narcissism, immaturity, and anti-social functioning.

Figure 3.10 This house was drawn by a 24-year-old female law student who demonstrated expansiveness on other measures.

15   Absence of a dividing line between the roof (or attic area) and the living area of the house:

(Ages 6 and older):
Reality/fantasy disturbance (e.g., schizophrenia) and usually reflects ideational turmoil and inadequate separation between fantasy (attic area) and reality (living area).

Figure 3.11 This house was drawn by a 58-year-old man who reported significant depressive and somatic symptoms.

16   Tile lines in the roof area:

All ages:
When the lines are horizontal, the individual may be experiencing pressures from ego-syntonic ideation. Conversely, when the lines are drawn vertically in the roof area, the individual is likely experiencing ego-dystonic, unacceptable ideation. Meticulous roof tiling reflects excessive obsessive-compulsive tendencies.

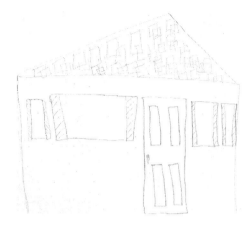

Figure 3.12 This house was drawn by a 20-year-old woman who had dropped out of college with the intention of resuming and was experiencing intense depression and anxiety.

17 Roof overhangs that protrude past wall lines:

All ages:
Paranoid ideation

Figure 3.13 This house was drawn by a 35-year-old female whose father had died a year and a half prior to the evaluation. She demonstrated defensiveness on the MMPI as indicated by an elevated K-scale, and her other test results suggested denial of depressive symptoms.

18 Roof/attic areas penetrated by other features (e.g., tree branches, sunrays, clouds):

All ages:
Rare and suggests disruptions that often reflect traumatic experiences.

Figure 3.14 This house was drawn by a 31-year-old female who presented with significant marital discord.

19 Absence of a front door:

All ages:
Rare and would reflect extreme isolation and mistrust. Treatment should be limited to pharmacological and crisis-intervention modalities as the relationship aspects of psychotherapy are too threatening.

Figure 3.15 This house was drawn by a 16-year-old male who had failed the 11th grade despite more than adequate cognitive abilities. He was noted to present with a façade of assurance while evaluation indicated overwhelming depression.

20 Doors without doorknobs, handles, or other indication of mechanism for opening:

All ages:
Resistance to self-exploration, limited insight, and the perception that therapy is threatening. Short-term and brief symptom-relief treatment modalities are within the capabilities of the individual.

Figure 3.16 This house was drawn by a 34-year-old man who demonstrated significant somatic concern and preoccupation with nutrition.

21   Doorknob size is disproportionate to size of door:

All ages:
Reflects accessibility to self-exploration in treatment. The larger the size of the doorknob, the greater the accessibility to treatment.

Figure 3.17 This house with a large doorknob was drawn by and 8-year-old boy who was seen in the context of a child custody and visitation rights evaluation.

22   Steps leading up to the door, pathway leading up to but not actually touching the baseline, and patio stones in front of the doorway:

All ages:
Other indication of inaccessibility to a relationship and treatment.

Figure 3.18 This house was drawn by a 55-year-old female who presented with generalized environmental stressors.

23 A second door:

All ages:
Ambivalence and anxiety regarding relationships and treatment. Brief, symptom-focused treatment is realistic for these individuals.

Figure 3.19 This house was drawn by a 17-year-old female who presented with depression and indicated anxiety related to libidinal pressures.

24 Doors with rounded top portions:

All ages:
Possibility of ideational pressure resulting from libidinal pressures.

Figure 3.20 This house was drawn by a 47-year-old female.

25 Other objects drawn inside the door outline (e.g., tree limb, bush, etc.):

All:
Rare and suggests sexual trauma experiences.

Figure 3.21 This house was drawn by a 16-year-old female who had a history of self-injurious behavior.

26 Breaks in the line(s) forming the wall(s):

All:
Consider intermittent or episodic breaks in reality testing

Figure 3.22 This house was drawn by a 17-year-old female who presented with behavioral acting out, anxiety, and depression.

27 Windows drawn within ½ inch of the roofline:

All:
Fear of anyone seeing inside, which ties in with severe pathology (e.g., paranoid and schizoaffective disorders). Windows are the opportunities to observe or be observed by others.

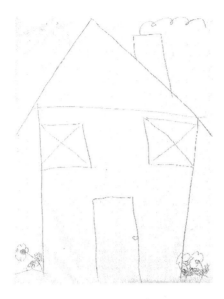

Figure 3.23 This house (Seen also in Item #17) is consistent with the guardedness previously discussed in the 35-year-old female drawer.

28   There is no roofline, and the windows extend up into the attic area:

All:
Suggests the pathology described in Item #27 with more definite severity.

Figure 3.24 This house was drawn by a 16-year-old female inpatient who complained of learning disability and presented with obsessive-compulsive tendencies and paranoid ideation.

29 Picture windows and windows placed within ½ inch of ground level:

All:
Exhibitionistic tendencies

Figure 3.25 This house was drawn by a 17-year-old male who presented with interpersonal difficulty with family members and acting out behavior.

30 Multiple vertical lines on the windows:

All:
Extreme caution and mistrust.

Figure 3.26 This house was drawn by a 9-year-old boy with longstanding disruptive behavior and impulsivity.

31 Crisscrossed lines in the window, including a single vertical and horizontal midline or crisscrossed diagonal lines:

All:
Poor impulse control. If the cross-hatching lines extend past the window outline, the lack of self-criticalness, lack of guilt and corresponding impulsivity are likely.

Figure 3.27 This house, which demonstrates lines extending past the window
    outlines, was drawn by a 12-year-old girl whose parents had di-
    vorced and continued to have conflict.

32 Windowpane lines that resembles a crucifix (i.e., the horizontal line crosses intersect the vertical line above its midpoint):

All:
Severe psychopathology, particularly when other indications of major mental illness exist. "Crucifix" windows are often drawn by individuals with paranoia and paranoid schizophrenia. The less appropriate the crucifix symbol is to the drawing (e.g., as eye pupils) the greater the likelihood of the presence of severe pathology. The degree of religiosity of the individual does not affect the scoring.

Figure 3.28 This house was drawn by a 26-year-old male who presented with paranoid ideation, behavioral acting out, and excessive religiosity.

33 Furniture inside the house:

Children (ages 6–12) and adolescents (ages 13 to 17):
Not uncommon for children and indicates a high level of preoccupation or concern for that room's significance.
Adults:
Rare and suggests more intense difficulties with regard to the dynamics raised by the furniture drawn.

34 A dining room table with no chairs:

All:
Accentuated nurture deprivation

35 Fences of all types:

All:
Guardedness, mistrust, paranoia, and poor social skills

36 Spiked Fence:

All:
Suggests aggressivity in addition to the interpretation of all fences in Item #35.

Figure 3.29 This spiked-fence lined house was drawn by a 21-year-old female
        who presented with anxiety, depression, and regressed behavior.

37 Mailboxes:

All:
Raises questions about identity (i.e., who lives here?)

38 Drainpipe along the wall of the house:

All:
*Immaturity, passive-aggressiveness and, particularly when water is
drawn coming out of the drainpipe, enuresis.*

39 Clouds or birds:

All:
Depressive overtones

40 The sun:

All:
Attachment to father/male figures.

Figure 3.30 This house drawn with a cloud and the sun was produced by a 38-year-old woman who reported depressive symptoms. She also included clouds and the sun in her Free Drawing and Kinetic Family Drawing.

41 Kites or balloons in the sky:

All:
Concealed dysphoria, external pressures, and insecurity.

42 Flowers or Shrubs around the house:

Females:
Emphasize the need to be seen as feminine. Often these individuals' resort to role-playing and manipulation in their relationships, particularly when the other person is a much older male.
Males:
Often struggling with their masculinity in conflicted and anxiety-producing ways.

Figure 3.31 The 26-year-old male who drew this house, discussed above in Item #32, showed evidence throughout the exam results of anger toward women and little identification with traditional male roles.

Follow-up inquiries for house drawings:

1   If any portion of the house does not fit on the page and is omitted (Item #5), inquire about the missing portion.

Tree Drawing Test Interpretations

The tree drawing can be administered on its own and is often done so in Japan (Le Corff et al., 2014), where it is shown to have stronger support as an independent measure. Its origins as a measure of personality (as opposed to Goodenough's analysis of tree drawings as a measure of nonverbal intelligence) began with its use as such by a vocational counselor in 1928 with the instruction, "Draw a fruit tree but not a Christmas tree." In 1928, Koch proposed the use of this method for clinical diagnosis.

The tree drawing is used to assess a deeper level of emotional history and personality functioning than is typically revealed in a human-figure drawing (Le Corff et al., 2014). The tree is theorized to represent life and growth, with its trunk symbolizing basic resources and ego strength (Handler, 2014). The trunk is also a representation of personality structure and emotional life. Trunks that open at the top may suggest impulsivity, while trunks that are larger at the base emphasize the importance of the past (Le Corff et al., 2014).

Branches represent a way of relating to the world and seeking satisfaction from the environment. Overly intellectual people tend to omit leaves and highly social people draw big loops. Flowers or fruit included in the tree may suggest narcissism, unless the drawer was instructed to draw fruit.

Roots in tree drawings have implications for reality testing, while "mutilations" (e.g., scars, knotholes, dead, or falling branches, etc.) can indicate trauma and have implications for self-perception. "Mutilations" including scars and knots on trees are correlated with history of trauma. The greater the number of mutilations, the longer the duration of abuse. Height of mutilation has been associated with age at which trauma occurred. Specifically, by dividing the height of the tree by the drawer's chronological age, a scale can be developed (e.g., an 18-year-old who draws a six-inch tree has represented 3-year increments of life with each inch).

Tree drawings provide an indication of disturbing ideation and excessive libidinal pressures throughout one's life span. Typically, the more unusual the tree markings, the more open they are to interpretation and the more the knowledge and experience of the interpreter comes into play. As stated previously, with all projectives, identical markings drawn by individuals of different age levels and/or different genders may require totally different interpretations.

Placement

The immediate concern with the tree drawing is its placement on the page. Trees drawn using the bottom edge of the page as a baseline occur most often with children and suggest that security needs are vital. The placement using the bottom of the page suggests that the need for environmental support is strong for this individual. The older the subject, the greater the significance given to a "baseline" tree and the more insecure he or she is. Usually, trees are drawn centered on the page. On occasion, the tree trunk is drawn close to either the right or left sides of the paper.

Strokes and Shading

The strength of the line quality (e.g., lightness or darkness) of the tree drawing is of extreme importance and the interpretation depends on how much of a difference in pencil pressure has occurred. Heavy shading coincides with depression, and the heavier and more extensive the shading, the greater the ongoing turmoil and the degree of depression. However, a major change in this interpretation occurs when the shading is done by holding the pencil horizontally, like an artist, to achieve the shading. This is generally suggestive of artificial, narcissistic, and manipulative tendencies and should not necessarily be interpreted in terms of a deep depression unless other depressive indicators are noted in the protocol. Obvious differences in pencil strength from one side of the tree drawing to the other denote possible fluctuating gender identification concerns or gender dysphoria.

Kinds of Trees

The type of tree drawn depends, in great part, on the expected foliage in the geographic area in which the testing takes place. For example, it is not unusual in the tropics for examinees to draw palm trees of various sorts. For children or adults who live or have grown up in colder climates, the pine or oak trees tend to be more common. However, the interpretation of distortions in the tree drawing should be consistent regardless of the type of tree drawn. For example, individuals who are extremely angry and prone to violence will draw a "spiked" tree regardless of whether it is a pine, fir, spruce, or palm tree. A "spike" tree includes pointed, dagger-like branches, roots, or leaf structures. Moreover, if a tree has a very pointed spike-like leaf at the top and, as very frequently happens, it touches the upper edge of the page, the possibility of aggressive sexual acting out should be considered. (Christmas trees obtained in July are often obtained from angry and depressed people.)

Leaf Structure

The leaf area provides a measure of cognitive organization and mental processes. If the leaf structure is contained inside a closed circular shape from one side of the trunk to the other, the heaviness of line is important. The presence of any broken twig or branch structure that protrudes from or breaks through the circular shape of the leaf area indicates that the likelihood of ongoing traumatic ideation should be considered. Also, the failure to complete the circle of leaf lines, with one or both sides left unattached to the branch section usually raises the question of unconscious, disturbing ideation disrupting conscious functioning by seeping out into awareness. When the child or adult has been hospitalized for psychological problems, and the above separation of the leaf structure from the trunk occurs, primary process turmoil is indicated.

If the leaf structure appears to cover the entire page from side to side and from the middle of the page to the top of the page, the expression of gross affective turmoil is being displayed. It is expected that the other psychological measures should give additional support to the presence of ongoing emotional turmoil. These individuals often appear agitated and verbose and could be experiencing hallucinatory or delusional phenomena. Extending leaf structure or trunk lines beyond the limits of the page always indicate poor planning, impaired judgment, a lack of self criticalness, tenuous libidinal and impulse control, and the strong likelihood of acting out in socially unacceptable ways.

When the leaf structure is drawn with pointed, arrow-like projections, the likelihood of unacceptable acting out anger is more likely. If the leaf structure is scribbled and disorganized, then the interpretation of ideational or cognitive turmoil would likely be accurate. If the tree leaves are more thorn-like rather than leaf-like, the presence of anger is both intense and threatening. These interpretations do not vary with age, education, gender, or ethnicity. In over 22,000 evaluations, the authors have never had a subject draw a log instead of a tree. While a log drawing per se has never been seen, "shattered" trees do occur. However, even when the trunk is shattered and the tree is broken off and touching the ground, the connecting line between the trunk and the portion that has fallen over is still connected. This occurs infrequently and generally from an extremely traumatized and seriously disturbed individual. Conversely, following the 1992 Hurricane disaster in Miami, Florida, in which damaged, shattered trees were prevalent, tree drawings by traumatized children and adults were not drawn as shattered.

Trunks

Regardless of the type of tree drawn, the length of the trunk, not including the leaf area structure, is viewed as representing the life span of the individual doing the drawing. Any distortions, hereafter referred to as trauma marks, whether they involve extensive roots or trunk marking, can therefore be related to the approximate age of the patient when some trauma or extreme difficulty occurred. For example, if the trunk is six inches long, the age of the subject in years is represented by those six inches, and each inch denotes one-sixth of that person's present chronological age. This helps in placing an age level for trauma-marks that may appear (e.g., the squirrel holes, trunk-slashes, or breaks in the exterior trunk lines). Also, the inside markings on the tree trunk can be of enormous importance. If there are a series of vertical lines throughout the tree trunk, the interpretation of life-long trauma and self-dissatisfaction can be easily made. For example, a drawing by a 14-year-old girl showed a spiral inside the trunk going left to right at approximately the nine-year level and another spiral that was reversed at the five-year level. The usual patterns tied in with the interpretation that trauma in the form of molestation had occurred at the five-year level and that she had started voluntary sexual behavior at approximately nine years of age. The drawing was obtained at age 14, when she was being evaluated for treatment following a second sexual trauma. The circular spiral configuration is rare.

A double line on one side of the tree trunk with a knot or a marking extended out from the tree usually indicates the subject's question of another's impotence as opposed to their own ineffectiveness (e.g., the husband of the female subject). The self-concept also comes into play. A tree with an extremely thin trunk with broken lines from top to bottom usually leads to the interpretation of a seriously impaired self-concept. In similar fashion, an excessively wide trunk drawn by a female would raise the question of role-play identification. Some palm trees, usually drawn by women, such as the royal palm, have a bulge at the bottom of the trunk, which ties in with pregnancy concerns for that individual.

It is not uncommon for the needy and critical person to draw a "lollipop" tree (i.e., a thin, stick-like trunk with a bare round circle at the top). Their needs to be taken care of are often expressed vis-à-vis a "lollipop" tree.

Roots

Vertical lines drawn as though the roots are seen, similar to a transparency, indicate extensive nurture deprivation. Excessive tree roots suggest insufficient, inadequate, and traumatic nurturance in infancy.

Branches

Broken off branches that appear on trunks below the leaf structures represent traumatic losses to the subjects at approximately the age indicated by the location of the break on the tree trunk. These losses commonly reflect the loss of a sibling, parent, grandparent, or of some other meaningful individual or psychosocial factor, either by death, divorce, abandonment, or incarceration.

Grass

Some subjects include vertical line drawings of grass around the tree structure either in tufts or in single lines at the ground level, which usually tie in with intense libidinal interests and pressures. In a child who has not been molested, the grass lines suggest an exaggerated insistence on being held by adults to the point where the child is seen as precocious and sometimes seductive or flirtatious with adults. In adults, the excessive grass along the bottom of the tree trunk line suggests that the affective and libidinal pressures are exaggerated.

Additions to the Tree

Often, the inclusion of "nice" things (e.g., a bird's nest, a swing or a tire swing from one of the limbs, Christmas presents) in the leaf structure can be interpreted as denial, and very likely as repression of rage and anger by the individual being evaluated. Of course, the interpretation of Christmas decorated trees would depend on the time of year where actual Christmas time might contaminate the interpretation. Similarly, the inclusion of "gifts" under the Christmas tree only emphasizes the denial of anger at conscious levels. The inclusion of additions in a thorn-like leaf structure is suggestive of exaggerated denial, repression, or even dissociation.

Individuals who draw apples or other fruit on their trees are expressing signs of nurture deprivation. If the fruit is drawn falling below the leaf structure or on the ground, the likelihood of depressed ideation or an unconscious dissatisfaction with self would be likely. This is also suggestive of a belief that nurturance is not forthcoming.

Regardless of right-handedness or left-handedness, exaggerations of line quality on the left side of the tree would be in keeping with internalized pressures, while exaggerations on the right-hand side of the page suggest that environmental factors are of primary importance in reflecting or emphasizing conscious disturbances.

Barren Trees

The totally bare and barren tree depicts the ultimate in depression and self-denigration. If the barren leaf area is combined with a heavily shaded trunk, depression and self-harm may be indicated as is often seen with potentially suicidal individuals. Interestingly enough, this type of tree is also drawn by the histrionic individuals who function covertly in terms often indicating the presence of consciously denied depression. The contrast between the depression and the denial itself and the casualness and goodness in which these individuals function, is a giveaway in terms of a diagnostic consideration.

Examples

For example, when evaluating two sisters, ages nine and eleven, who had been fondled by their stepfather, each child separately drew a house with a tree going through and covering the doorway of the house. The examiner asked a third sister, age sixteen, to examine the drawing of one of the younger siblings for five minutes and then try to duplicate it from memory. After five minutes, the examiner removed the drawing from her view and asked her to redraw it. The elder sister drew the house and then the tree, nowhere near the doorway. In fact, she had not accused the stepfather of molestation but had reported the younger sisters' involvement. It appeared obvious to the examiner that the tree as a male symbol was placed appropriately by her. No molestation had occurred with the sixteen-year-old sister; however, the tree drawings of the younger siblings helped to confirm allegations of molestation. Additional confirmation of these findings occurred during the trial and the accused pedophile was convicted of sexual battery on a minor.

Tree Drawing Test Scores

33 Trees placed within 1/2 inch of the bottom edge of the paper:

Children and adolescents (ages 6–17):
Appropriate security needs.
Adults (ages 18 and older):
Insecurity and dependence on external support. The older the individual, the greater the clinical significance of the insecurity and dependence

34 The leaf structure extends beyond the limits of the page:

All: Poor judgment, ideational turmoil, impaired planning and lack of forethought, a lack of self-criticalness, and a strong likelihood of acting out in socially unacceptable ways.

Figure 3.32 This tree was drawn by the 16-year-old female described in Item #28, who also was evaluated as having ideational disturbance.

35 Heavy or dark line shading:

All: Depression. The heavier or darker the line shading, the greater the degree of depression.

Figure 3.33 This tree was drawn by a 13-year-old female who had experienced her parents' divorce as traumatic. She indicated depressive symptoms, including overt crying throughout the evaluation.

36 Shading made with the pencil held horizontally, like an artist would:

All: Narcissistic and manipulative tendencies. Not indicative of depression.

37 "Spiked" tree includes pointed or dagger-like branches, roots, or leaf structures.

All: Extreme anger and violence proneness; If the dagger-like portion goes off of the top or sides of the page, consider aggressive acting out.

Figure 3.34 This spiked tree was drawn by the same 53-year-old woman who drew the house featured in Item #6.

37b Leaves that are more like thorns like than leaf-like:

All: Strong presence of anger that is both intense and threatening to erupt.

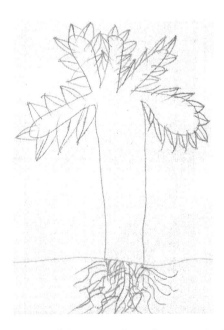

Figure 3.35 This tree was drawn by a severely disturbed 17-year-old male inpatient who was noted to be manipulative, paranoid, and glib, and showed indications of severe pathology on objective evaluation measures.

37c Christmas trees, regardless of season

Anger and depression

Figure 3.36 This Christmas tree was drawn by a 7-year-old boy who was evaluated, along with his parents and his 10-year-old brother, in the context of a custody evaluation.

37d "Shattered" or grossly disfigured trees

All: Rare and suggest trauma and serious disturbance

37e "Lollipop" trees (i.e., a thin, stick-like trunk with a bare round circle at the top)

Dependence, neediness, and accentuated need to be taken care of; consider chemical dependency, immaturity and substance abuse.

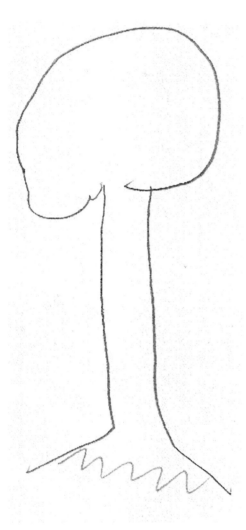

Figure 3.37 This lollipop tree was drawn by a 31-year-old man who was involved in a motor vehicle accident and showed cognitive decline on evaluation. He reported concern about the impact of the accident and his resulting level of functioning on his marriage.

38 Any distortions on the trunk (e.g., squirrel holes, knot holes, vertical lines, trunk slashes or breaks in the exterior trunk lines):

All: Suggestive of trauma; the length of the trunk is viewed as representing the lifespan of the individual. For example, if a trunk is six inches long, the age of the individual in years is divided by six to suggest the age at time of trauma.

Figure 3.38 This tree was drawn by a 12-year-old girl and illustrates vertical trunk lines, a hole in the trunk, and breaks in the exterior trunk lines. The girl's parents were divorced when she was approximately six years old and had ongoing conflict.

39 Roots:

All: Usually reflect insufficient, inadequate, and traumatic nurturance in infancy.

Figure 3.39 This tree with roots was drawn by a 47-year-old woman who presented with depression, anxiety, and difficulty controlling anger. There were signs throughout her results of nurture deprivation and anger directed at her mother. The fruit drawn in this tree is consistent with an interpretation of nurture deprivation. (See Item #65).

40 Any broken branch structure that protrudes from the leaf area:

All: Indicates the presence of ongoing primary process ideation. Leaf structures provide a measure of the individual's cognitive organization and mental processes.

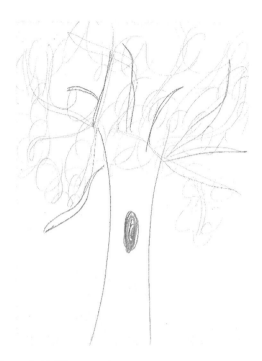

Figure 3.40 This tree drawing demonstrates broken branches protruding from the leaf structure (Item #60) and Scribbled and disorganized leaf structure (Item #61). The 24-year-old female examinee presented with depression and significant self-dissatisfaction as well as relationship difficulties.

41   Scribbled and disorganized leaf structures:

All: Ideational or cognitive turmoil

42   Arrow-like projection leaves:

All: Acting out anger.

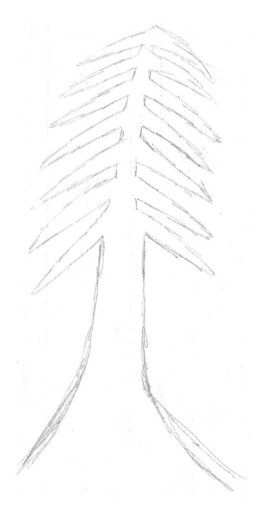

Figure 3.41 This tree with arrow-like projections was drawn by a 31-year-old
woman who had intense anger toward her siblings.

43 Broken off branches that appear on trunks below the leaf structures:

All: Often represent traumatic losses at approximately the ages indicated by the location of the branch on the trunk. Common losses could be loss of parent, grandparent, sibling via psychosocial factors like death, divorce, injury, illness, incarceration, or abandonment.

Figure 3.42 This tree was drawn by a 41-year-old man who was in the process of obtaining a divorce and was seen for a custody evaluation.

44   Grass around the tree:

All: Intense libidinal interests and pressures. In these individuals, affective and libidinal pressures are intensified

Figure 3.43 This tree was drawn by a 17-year-old female who presented with depression and was noted to have indications of libidinal pressure throughout the evaluation, including decline in grades after elementary school, expression of the need for a boyfriend, and "phobic" responses to the sexual areas of the Rorschach cards.

45 Addition of "nice" things on or under the leaf structure (e.g., bird's nest, swing, tire-swing, Christmas ornaments or presents):

All: Excessive denial and repression of anger or rage.

Figure 3.44 This tree with a nest of birds was drawn by the 20-year-old described in Item #17 who presented with depression and anxiety. There were several indications in the evaluation results suggesting difficulty controlling anger, including the spiked quality of this tree drawing.

46 Apples or other fruit drawn on the tree:

All: Nurture deprivation, depressed ideation and unconscious dis-satisfaction with self

46a Fruit that has fallen on the ground:

All: Belief that nurturance is not forthcoming.

Figure 3.45 This tree was drawn by the 9-year-old boy discussed in Item #31 with disruptive behavior and impulsivity. The examiner noted intense sibling rivalry, which may have contributed to his acting out behavior. Several indications of paranoia were also noted throughout test results.

77 A barren tree:

All: Expresses the ultimate in depression and self-denigration

Figure 3.46 This barren tree was drawn by a 61-year-old man whose MMPI profile indicated significant depression and somatic concerns. He had a history of rheumatic fever for which he received compensation from the military.

47a Barren trees combined with a darkly shaded trunk area:

All: Suggests self-harm potential is high and hospitalization may be necessary

Figure 3.47 This barren, shaded tree was drawn by a 17-year-old female who reported self-consciousness due to motor impairment and difficulty with assertiveness.

Person Drawing Test

Please proceed to Chapter IV for a more thorough discussion of the Person Drawing Test, which can be administered alone or in conjunction with the House-Tree-Person sequence.

4 Draw-A-Person Test

Machover's (1949) system, much like the current system, was based on a large number of clinical observations to which she applied interpretations that were heavily influenced by psychoanalytic theory. Several of the procedures of Machover's method were adopted for the CCPAM. Similar to Machover's instructions, the current system involves directing examinees to draw a person, draw another person of the opposite sex, and answer questions about the human figures in the inquiry phase. Machover did not advise imposing the structure of the current system, which includes the instruction to draw whole people "from head to toe." Machover (1949) commented that examinees who draw the head of a person only were usually encouraged to complete their drawings, and that the exact wording of the instructions was undefined because it was unclear which instruction would promote the most projection.

Machover also advised examiners to emphasize to the examinee that effort, rather than artistic ability, was the purpose of the task. Machover commented on adult males being heavily represented in her sample as an artifact of her clinical work and reported, "Though some of the assumptions may lack experimental verification, they have proved clinically valid" (1949, p. 34). Some of her cases were compared to their Rorschach interpretations. The authors of the current system sought to advance the empirical validation of the scoring system with the protocols of multiple measures from males and females of a wide age range.

Machover (1949) provided general commentary on interpreting qualities of drawings, including size, placement on the page, speed of drawing, and line quality, among others. A more thorough discussion of various body parts was also included with interpretations of what various qualities may mean; however, the system lacks a well-defined, user-friendly scoring system and relies heavily on subjective judgment.

In terms of comparison of specific interpretations between Machover's system and the CCPAM, several similarities exist. For example, as in the CCPAM, Machover noted the omission of pupils from the eyes as being

DOI: 10.4324/9781003308799-4

clinically significant and interpreted this as the examinee having a vague perception of the world. Both systems agree that accentuation of the ears indicates various interpretations, including sensitivity or paranoia. There is also agreement between the systems on the presence of detailed hair representing sexual ideation. Machover discussed the nose as a phallic symbol, with its treatment in drawings having sexual connotations, while the CCPAM identifies small noses to represent general feelings of inadequacy, powerlessness, or self-dissatisfaction.

Similar interpretations are made in both systems in relation to the neck. Machover interpreted short or absent necks as a sign of immaturity, irrationality, and impulsivity while the CCPAM similarly interprets stubbornness and lack or planning or forethought. Both systems view separation between the head and the body as indicative of severe pathology; however, Machover's system accounts for this separation with a long neck while the CCPAM scores an actual separation or break in the neckline.

The absence of or concealment of hands is interpreted by both systems as evasiveness and guilt, particularly related to masturbation. Both systems give similar treatment to fingers, with fists indicating aggression, missing fingers indicating castration anxiety, and talon-like fingers indicating paranoia, per Machover, and aggression in the CCPAM.

In both systems, buttons and pockets are associated with dependency features and ties are considered a sexual symbol dealing with inadequacy. Dark lines on human figure drawings are related to anger and hostility in the CCPAM while Machover attributed shading to anxiety. The order in which the male and female figures are drawn is important in both systems, with an interpretation of disruption in gender identification when examinees first draw a figure of the opposite sex from their own.

In contrast to CCPAM, which includes the option to ask follow up questions about each drawing, Machover's method involved asking the examinee to make up a story about each human figure drawing, or alternatively, asking questions about the drawings if the examinee resisted production of a story. Similar to the inquiry phase of CCPAM, Machover's "Associations (1949, p. 31)" phase allows for follow up questions, as appropriate, to the standard questions. Compared to the CCPAM, which attempts to allow for more projection, Machover's system included more direct and specific questions related to family and education background as well as sexual activity, and both systems inquire about emotional state and physical appraisal (i.e., best and worst parts of the body).

Naglieri et al. (1991) Draw A Person: Screening Procedure for Emotional Disturbance was developed as a brief measure for use with children and adolescents ages 6 to 17 years old. The Draw A Person technique requires examinees to produce separate man, woman, and self drawings. The authors cited the primary objectives of the system to include ease and objectivity of scoring, contemporary norms with a representative sample of the United States, empirically supported distinction between "normal and disturbed populations" (p.3), and evaluation of both cognitive and emotional functioning. Naglieri and colleagues (1991) proposed the use of global interpretation of drawings as an indication of adjustment, rather than interpretation of specific items to support specific issues or diagnoses. The 55 scoring items are evaluated based on dimensions, placement, and specified qualities of the drawings.

Several items of the DAP: SPED (1991) are similar to items on CCPAM. Both systems include scoring criteria based on size; however, the DAP:SPED evaluates dimensions of human figure drawings, while the CCPAM qualitatively evaluates the size of the male and female drawings in comparison to one another. Transparencies, in which body parts are visible through clothing or through other body parts, and nude or semi-nude figures are scored on both systems. Vacant eyes or omitted pupils are scored on both systems as are diverted gazes, with the DAP:SPED scoring right or left gaze and the CCPAM scoring downward gaze. The DAP:SPED includes scores related to shading of several different body parts, while CCPAM includes a score for dark lines on any part of the drawing. The DAP:SPED includes scores for a frowning mouth, "slash mouth," and the presence of teeth, while the CCPAM includes a score for an open mouth or the absence of teeth. Both systems include criteria for hands drawn in a fist and pointed or talon-like fingers.

Person Drawing Scores:

The following section contains the scorable items, interpretive considerations, and drawing examples (where available) for the person drawings. Note that these are applicable to both person drawings completed by the participant. Please see Appendix A for a brief scoring key to be used when analyzing drawings (Figures 4.1–4.21).

79 *[Behavioral Score]: If applicable given the participant's self-described gender identity, other individual factors, and referral issue(s), the participant draws a figure of the opposite gender first.

Male or Female: Gender confusion or dysphoria.

Figure 4.1 On the left is the drawing of a male figure drawn first by a 15-year-old Hispanic female whose father had passed away suddenly two-and-a-half years prior to administration. She subsequently developed somatic and depressive symptoms, followed by two suicide attempts with inpatient hospitalization. In this context, the primacy of the male figure could reflect the persisting preoccupation with loss of her father, while the female figure is secondary and shown with sullen affect (consistent with the young lady's affect during administration). Also note the male figure is visibly larger than the female figure, reflecting item 80 (below).

Figure 4.2 (shared caption with Figure 4,1, which should be positioned to the left of Figure 4.2).

80 Comparison of the two figures' sizes

All: Much larger figures suggest the gender of the larger figure is more threatening and aggressive than the smaller figure. The significance includes the self-described gender of the individual in terms of identification with the larger figure (aggressor) or smaller figure (possible victim of aggression).

Figure 4.3 On the left is the drawing of a male person, which was the first drawn by a 14-year-old Hispanic male whose father died in a work-related accident two-and-a-half years prior to administration. Note the dark lines that exemplify item 92, which suggests consideration of anger or hostility. The young man's history was remarkable for getting into fights at school following his father's death. On the right, his second person drawing, of a female, is notably larger than the male figure, which could reflect feeling threatened or intimidated by females.

Figure 4.4 (shared caption with Figure 4.3, which should be positioned to the left of Figure 4.4).

81   Ear(s) that are accentuated (in size and/or attention to detail)

All: Interpersonal sensitivity, mistrust, and possible paranoia

82   Detailed hair

All: Excessive sexual ideation

83   Eyes without pupils

All: Lack of insight and possible primal scene trauma

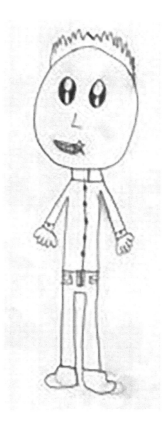

Figure 4.5 These figures were drawn by a 12-year-old girl who, along with her parents, was in a car accident resulting in traumatic brain injury and persistent increased clinginess with her parents (who were also injured in the accident), fear of something bad happening to them, nightmares, and wanting to sleep in the same room as her parents. Notably, both figures are lacking pupils, reflecting preoccupation and trauma around parental relations.

Figure 4.6 (shared caption with Figure 4.5, which should be positioned to the left of Figure 4.6).

84 Eyes with pupils facing down

All: Anxiety related to sex

Figure 4.7 This drawing of a female was the first drawn by a 12-year-old Hispanic boy whose father had died two-and-a-half years prior to administration. The anxiety suggested by the downward facing pupils was consistent with self-report and parent-rating scales that yielded elevations on scaled related to anxiety and fears, as well as the man's history of increased anxiety and isolation following his father's death. Also note the "lollipop head" illustrative of item 85 (below).

85 Lollipop heads

All: Role-playing tendencies
(See above illustration.)

86   No necks or thick necks (>1/3 of the width of the head)

All: Stubbornness, lack of planning or forethought

Figure 4.8 This male drawing was drawn second by a 12-year-old Hispanic male with a history of defiance and verbal aggression toward his mother following the death of his father. The boy had a history of academic underachievement despite having an Average-range IQ. The missing neck in his drawing is suggestive of lack of planning and forethought, which would likely manifest in academic and home settings.

87 Heads/necks that are disconnected from the shoulders

All: Poor reality testing and severe pathology

Figure 4.9 This male figure was person drawn by a six-year-old boy with difficulty focusing, regulating his energy, and making friends. The impaired reality testing suggested by the lack of connection between the head and body was consistent with objective findings indicating that in comparison to most boys his age, at times he seemed out of touch with reality and unaware of others, talked to himself, seemed confused, and acted strangely. Results yielded a new diagnosis of Autism Spectrum Disorder.

88   Nude of semi-nude (no top or no bottom clothing) figures

All: Severe pathology (e.g., schizophrenia), exhibitionism, and narcissism).

Figure 4.10 This male drawing was drawn by an eight-year-old boy with a
history of auditory processing disorder, reading and writing difficulties, and escalating oppositional behavior. Test results confirmed
a Reading Disability and also revealed that he tended to
decompensate behaviorally and emotionally with his parents,
especially his father, of whom he was afraid and particularly scared
by yelling.

89 Transparencies (seeing the body through clothing)

Children (ages 6–12):
No interpretation
Adolescents and adults (ages 13 and older):
Schizophrenia

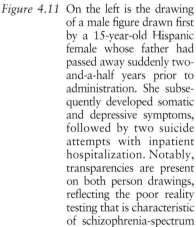

Figure 4.11 On the left is the drawing of a male figure drawn first by a 15-year-old Hispanic female whose father had passed away suddenly two-and-a-half years prior to administration. She subsequently developed somatic and depressive symptoms, followed by two suicide attempts with inpatient hospitalization. Notably, transparencies are present on both person drawings, reflecting the poor reality testing that is characteristic of schizophrenia-spectrum disorders.

Figure 4.12 (shared caption with Figure 4.11, which should be positioned to the left of Figure 4.12).

90a Four-fingered hand

Males:
Anxiety regarding emasculation
Females:
No interpretation

90b Pointed or talon-like fingers

All: Aggressivity.

Figure 4.13 Drawn by a 30-year-old female with Borderline Personality
Disorder, the pointed/talon-like fingers of this female figure reflect
aggressive tendencies consistent with her history of verbal aggression directed toward family members, friends, paramours, cow-
orkers, and supervisors, as well as feeling "enraged, angry,
hysterical, and trapped." Also note the dark lines, further suggesting anger and hostility (as scored per Item 92, below).

90c Fists

All: Aggressivity and passive-aggressive tendencies

91 Wrist lines

All: Depression and possible self-harm.

Figure 4.14 The 30-year-old female who drew this female figure with wrist lines reflecting her own history of self-harm that began when she was 12 years old.

92   Dark lines

All: Anger and hostility (verbal or physical)

Figure 4.15 These figures were drawn by a 12-year-old girl who, along with her parents, was in a car accident resulting in traumatic brain injury and persistent listlessness, personality change, memory problems, distractibility, nightmares, fears, crying spells, and separation anxiety. The dark lines are suggestive of anger and hostility.

Figure 4.16 (shared caption with Figure 4.15, which should be positioned to the left of Figure 4.16).

93a Buttons

Children (ages 6–12):
No interpretation
Adolescents and adults (ages 13 and older):
Accentuated dependency features

93b A tie drawn on the male figure ·

Adult males (ages 18 and older):
Insecurity, inadequacy, and sexual concerns.
Females and younger males (ages 17 and younger):
No interpretation

93c Shirt pockets or pants pockets

Children (ages 6–12):
No interpretation
Adolescents and adults (ages 13 and older):
Exaggerated dependency features.

93d High heels or overly detailed shoes

All: Obsessive-compulsive defenses and passive-aggressive tendencies.

Figure 4.17 The 11-year-old male who drew this male figure had a history of Autism Spectrum Disorder and Attention-Deficit Hyperactivity Disorder, and he had been psychiatrically hospitalized twice in the preceding six months for suicidal ideation and aggression toward family members. The obsessive-compulsive tendencies suggested by the attention to detail in the drawn figure's shoes is consistent with collateral reports that he had difficulty coping with setbacks and changes and, "He tries to control everything." Also note the dark lines indicative of hostility, which is consistent with his history of aggression.

93e Purses or briefcases

All: Feelings of inadequacy and covert aggressivity

94   Open mouths or mouths without teeth

All: Exaggerated oral dependency needs, cutting sarcasm, and addiction-proneness.

Figure 4.18 Drawn by a 14-year-old female, this male figure's open mouth is suggestive of oral dependency needs. She was adopted in the United States from Russia when she was six months old, and was noted to have a history of anxiety, verbal and physical aggression, and extreme tantrums in which she would destroy or discard others' personal items. Note that her drawing is suggestive of addiction-proneness, as is her history of aggression and conduct problems.

95 Facial scars

All: Deviant dependency features and antisocial tendencies; item should not be scored if the examinee has a facial scar.

Figure 4.19 Drawn by the same 14-year-old female described in Item 94, above, the facial scars seen on her drawing of a female reflect deviant dependency features and antisocial tendencies. As previously reported, she had been adopted at age six months and had a long history of engaging in disruptive and destructive behavior, usually in response to being asked to do something she did not want to do (e.g., cleaning her room).

96 Small noses (≤1/6 of the size of the face)

All: Feelings of inadequacy, powerlessness, and self-dissatisfaction.

Figure 4.20 On the left is the drawing of a male figure drawn first by a 15-year-old Hispanic female whose father had passed away suddenly two-and-a-half years prior to administration. She subsequently developed somatic and depressive symptoms, followed by two suicide attempts with inpatient hospitalization. Consistent with her history and remarks such as, "Why do I exist, no one cares if I am existing," the small noses featured on both drawings reflect the feelings of worthlessness characteristic of depression.

Figure 4.21 (shared caption with Figure 4.20, which should be positioned to the left of Figure 4.21).

5   Kinetic Family Drawing Test

Administration procedures for the Kinetic Family Drawing (KFD) are described in Chapter 2. The examinee is simply instructed, "Draw a picture of your family doing something." While drawing, the examiner should note any significant observations regarding the examinee's approach and behavior, as well as any countertransference experiences evoked within the examiner. Following completion of this drawing and any other projective drawings that may be administered, the examinee should be asked to describe what is happening in the KFD.

According to Burns and Kaufman (1972), their development of the Kinetic Family Drawing (Burns, & Kaufman, 1970) was designed with the intention of adding movement or activity to family drawings in order to demonstrate the child drawer's emotions related to self and relationships. The authors provided case examples of clinical and nonclinical children and discussed the overtness of interpretable information provided in their drawings, that is, the openness with which many children approach this task, possibly in contrast to clinical interviews. Burns and Kaufman (1970, 1972) direct administrators to ask the child examinee to draw the members of his or her family as whole people, rather than as cartoons or stick people. They also advise administrators to leave the room while children complete their Kinetic-Family-Drawing, returning periodically to monitor and encourage as needed; however, this practice may preclude collection of important qualitative and process data.

In developing their scoring system, Burns and Kaufman (1970, 1972) made interpretations based on characteristics of individual figures, actions or interactions between figures, "styles," "evasions," and symbols. Some of their content scores are similar to those in the CCPAM system free drawing, though several of the symbols are interpreted differently by the two systems. Kaufman and Burns (1970, 1972) interpreted drawings including beds to indicate sexual concerns or depressive symptoms. The CCPAM interprets free drawings of beds to indicate sensual concerns and tendencies toward somatization and manipulation through somatic complaints. This interpretation is more specific than general depressive symptoms; however, it can be clinically subsumed under depression. Burns

DOI: 10.4324/9781003308799-5

and Kaufman (1970) interpret drawings that include bikes to suggest masculine striving. In the CCPAM, a bike would not receive interpretation unless it met criteria for any of the items pertaining to vehicle qualities. Drawings that include cats were interpreted by Burns and Kaufman (1970) as ambivalence and involvement in conflict while the CCPAM interprets free drawings of any furry animal as indicative of unmet affective needs. Drawings, including fire, were interpreted by Burns and Kaufman (1970) as a need for warmth or love and the recognition of the drawer that love may turn into hate. The CCPAM interprets flames or flame-like features to suggest covert guilt regarding real or fantasized sexual behavior. Burns and Kaufman's (1970) interpretations of flower drawings are generally positive and include love of beauty and growth, feminine identification, interest in nurturance, and need for love. Conversely, the CCPAM interprets flowers as indicating intense affective needs and, when drawn lining a house by females, as suggestive of a need to be seen as feminine and a tendency toward role-playing and manipulation. When males draw flowers around a house, the interpretation is struggle with masculinity and related anxiety. The CCPAM interprets stars drawn in the sky or on an astrological chart as suggestive of psychosis and schizoaffective disorders, while Burns and Kaufman (1970) interpreted stars as suggesting physical or emotional deprivation or pain. The sun is a symbol of unresolved paternal attachment in the free and house drawings of the CCPAM. Burns and Kaufman (1970) incorporated positioning of figures in relation to the sun into their interpretations, with figures facing toward the sun indicating a need for warmth and acceptance and figures facing away from the sun indicating feelings of rejection. Burns and Kaufman (1970) interpreted train drawings as preoccupation with power, while the CCPAM interprets trains as suggesting atypical erotic ideation or behavior. Burns and Kaufman (1972) provided frequency data for some of their scoring items, but no other quantitative analysis.

Handler (2014) cited a lack of research on the KFD, noting that its use and interpretive material has been primarily clinical. Handler and others have recommended "Impressionistic Analysis" of the whole drawing before analysis of its structures and components.

Kinetic Family Drawing Test Interpretations

In the Kinetic Family Drawing test, the subject is asked to draw each member of his or her family engaged in some form of activity. The material obtained involves manifest and latent content to the drawings, and interpretation should include the possible significance of omissions and exaggerations. Particularly for children, where examinees place drawings of themselves in relation to drawings of the parental figures and siblings and the size and line quality of the figures drawn offer a great deal of information about the intensity or lack of relationships.

For example, in a family custody evaluation, a child drew herself in the lower right-hand corner of the page near her mother drawing and drew her father facing away from them in the upper left-hand gradient of the page.

The order in which the family members are drawn by examinees of all ages is also extremely significant. Typically, in a child's family drawing, the father is drawn first and then the mother, so that any variation on this is open to interpretation. The placement of the family and the figure size of the family members must also be considered. While the siblings may be older, the person producing the drawing may make himself larger. Omissions of any particular family member would be of enormous significance. Any omission of a family member suggests serious ideational disturbance involving the missing member.

The familial activities depicted also must be interpreted, particularly in terms of the interaction between the person being evaluated and the remainder of the family. The touching, in the drawing, of one family member with another has to be interpreted in terms of close attachment and intimacy, particularly if it is a child drawing himself or herself holding hands with the parent.

The implements depicted as being used by the family members in their activities project significant information about the examinee being tested. For example, one boy drew his family engaged in various activities. He drew himself fishing, holding a fishing pole while, the father was drawn watering the garden, holding a water hose. His and his father's use of male (phallic) symbols, while the mother and sister were not drawn in the same involvement, were interpreted as an identification with the father.

Cooking implements depicted in the KFD test, particularly if used by the mother, are seen in terms of the nurture received from the mother figure. An adult female who draws herself cooking and simultaneously throwing a pot across the room sees the female and mother roles as dissatisfying. This individual is angry about the responsibilities involved in fulfilling these roles and gets little gratification from serving as mother, feeling angry, depressed, and totally negative.

Another example of role dissatisfaction occurred with a woman who drew her family including a number of male siblings. All of the family members were drawn participating in recreational activities except for herself, whom she drew cleaning and making beds. The interpretation was seen as an angry demonstration of the insignificance of the female role for her and her family members, as she had to take care of other family members and do chores while they enjoyed themselves. Masochism, immaturity, subservience, and poor self-concept also come into play as well as the representation of being pushed into a mother role as a child and being responsible for siblings.

Adult patients, male or female, who when asked to draw a picture of their family draw a picture of the family they grew up in (family of origin) as opposed to their present day spouse and children are rejecting of their marriage and children and exhibiting regressive behavior through an almost conscious wish to be out of all responsibility and to be taken care of again by his or her own family.

Location of the various family members on the page is significant. If, for example, the family is drawn with a mother and child at one end of the paper and the father at the other side of the page, it certainly has to be interpreted as distant from the family constellation. If family members are drawn directly above or below one another as opposed to side by side, those family members seen as dominant, in charge, or important in some ongoing manner would be drawn above the remaining family members.

A significant change in pencil shading with no seemingly apparent reason may reveal affective disorders. Heavy pencil shading indicates the possibility of depression and dissatisfaction. The heavier the pencil shading, the more severe the depression. If the shading becomes too light, it suggests anxiety and depression that may not be in awareness. What areas are shaded is also important. Excessive shading of the head area (e.g., hair, forehead, face) should tie in with conscious anxiety and ideation that is disturbing.

Absence of a particular feature must always be considered as meaningful. The absence of a nose, pupils in the eyes, ears, or the emphasis of ears on one particular figure, where other figures are not missing these features or do not have these emphases For example, the absence of ears on the mother figure, while other family members are drawn with ears intact, would imply the mother's inattentiveness. The absence of pupils usually involves concern with the sexual behavior of parents and primal scene types of anxiety. Crossed eyes on figures would imply a humorous attempt to mask issues with phallic or masculine sexuality.

The family drawing is of particular importance in custody issues. Regardless of what a child may say, what he or she does with either parent in terms of the drawing should carry a great deal of weight. The child will often give lip service to his or her expressions of interest that may not be in accord with the material obtained. Divorce is very traumatic for children. They feel forced to make a choice of one parent over the other and may verbally try to remain neutral or loyal to both. The psychological evaluation usually obtains, either verbally or symbolically, the child's desire and preference that the parents stay married and together; however, the KFD test will furnish evidence of parental preference or attachment.

The interpretation stated earlier for adults who draw their family of origin instead of their nuclear family is reemphasized when these drawings occur during custody evaluations (Figures 5.1–5.5).

Kinetic Family Drawing Test Scores:

72 Order in which family members are drawn

All: Signifies the order of psychological importance the family member has to the individual

73 The placement of the figures on the paper and proximity to the individual's figure

All: Proximity to the individual's figure is interpreted as attachment (if within ½ inch) or rejection (if >1.5 inches away)

Figure 5.1 This drawing was made by a girl who was five years and 11 months old at the time of administration. When she was three, her mother moved away and did not see the girl for several months, resulting in expressed confusion, defiance, trichotillomania, and regression in toileting. The girl drew herself first, on the far left, followed by her mother, father, and "sister" (she did not have a sister). The distance between the figures reflects the girl's feelings of rejection, while the family's engagement in gardening together (in the context of her history) suggests fantasized closeness (i.e., a wish for cooperation and nurture within her family) as described in item 76 (see below).

73a Figures facing away from each other

All: Rejection

74 Parental figures drawn smaller than children

All: A lack of parental maturity, parental inconsistency, and a lack of adequate nurture and limit-setting by parents; Parental figures should be larger than sibling or self-presentation.

74a Adults who draw self smaller than own children

Adults (ages 18 and older):
Rejection of adult, parental role

75   Omission of any particular family member

All: Critical; Serious ideational disturbance involving the missing member, including the individual himself or herself.

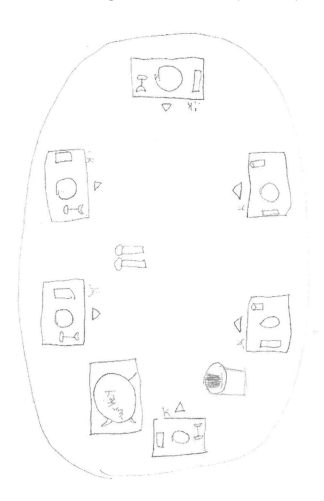

Figure 5.2 Note that this drawing has been altered to erase the first initial of each family member's name and protect confidentiality. Drawn by a 14-year-old adopted female indicates severe disturbance suggestive of alienation and consistent with her history of anxiety, aggression, and conduct problems.

75a Adults who draw family of origin instead of spouse and children

Adults (ages 18 and older):
Rejection of marriage and parenting responsibilities; They are exhibiting
regressive behavior with a wish to be taken care of by their own parents.

76 Family group activities involving all figures drawn

All: Fantasized or artificial closeness

Figure 5.3 This drawing was made by a girl who was five years and 11 months
old at the time of administration. Her parents separated when she
was three and she did not see her mother for several months, and had
been seeing her mother every other weekend since then. The girl had
continued to demonstrate confusion, defiance, trichotillomania, and
regression in toileting. The girl drew herself first, on the far left,
followed by her mother, father, and "sister" (she did not have a
sister). She described the figures as gardening together, and she
depicted seeds, sprouts, and small plants being watered. In the context of her history, these features raise consideration for fantasized
closeness with family members.

77 Heavy shading

All: Depression and conscious self and other dissatisfaction

Figure 5.4 This drawing was made by a 12-year-old girl who, along with her
parents, was in a car accident resulting in traumatic brain injury and
persistent listlessness, personality change, memory problems, distractibility, nightmares, fears, crying spells, and separation anxiety.
The heavy shading suggestive of depression and self and other dissatisfaction was consistent with the girl's history as well as self-report
and parent-rating inventories yielding elevations on scales related to
reality distortion, psychological discomfort, somatic complaints, and
withdrawal.

78a Fishing poles

All: Sexual symbols; Poles drawn extending off of the edge of the paper
suggest sexual acting out by the family member holding the pole.

78b Cooking implements

All: Depict nurturance from the person using them.

78c Absence of chairs around a dining table or not enough chairs to
accommodate all family members drawn

All: Frustrated dependency needs

Figure 5.5 This drawing was made by a 30-year-old female with a history of trauma, mood dysregulation, relationship problems, and daily marijuana use. She lived in a different state than her parents and two adult brothers and frequently referred to herself as "alone down here." Her drawing depicts a line between her family and herself, whom she described as "alone and depressed." The lack of chairs reflects her perceived lack of nurture and unmet dependency needs.

78d Swimming activities

All: Dependency features

78e Mirror(s) or Phone(s)

All: Narcissism and rejection by the figure using the mirror or the phone

6 Free Drawing Test

Free Drawing Test Interpretations

The Free Drawing should follow the KFD as a means of applying a projective measure with no structure or meaning. Similar to Card 16 (the blank card) of the Thematic Apperception Test, the subject is not given a stimulus figure with which to yield information. As such, the Free Drawing is a superb addition to the psychological battery.

Artistic ability does not factor into interpretation. It does not matter how well the drawing is done. What is drawn and how it is completed are much more important. In fact, it has been the experience of the first author to see professional artists handle resistance by indicating some form of dissatisfaction with the instruments available such as, "this paper isn't right for drawing" or "I don't use pencils." Examinees have also handled the Free Drawing with statements that attempt humor such as, "Of course, you can't sell this" or "I want royalties." These types of assertions would also be interpreted as evidence of narcissism, negativism, and interpersonal mistrust.

Since it is up to the examinee to decide what to draw, the more unusual the Free Drawing, the more pertinent the information obtained. With the Free Drawing, it is very important that the instructions are simply stated as "please draw anything at all." Do not ask the examinee to "draw anything [they] want" or "anything [they] would like." The instructions should be totally ambiguous. If the subject tries to press for structure by asking for more information (e.g., "What should I draw?"), the response should always be, "Draw anything at all, except a house, a tree, or a person."

Tempo and sequence, again, are important in interpreting the Free Drawing test, as it is the drawing test that typically produces the greatest indication of anxiety and concern. The lack of structure is difficult for examinees to deal with, so that its interpretation must include the speed with which it was drawn in contrast to the other drawing tests. Any additional time spent on the Free Drawing in contrast to rapid results for the other drawings suggests that whatever has been drawn is heavily

DOI: 10.4324/9781003308799-6

loaded with affective significance. This drawing test is very difficult for people who are anxious about keeping their ideation masked. For example, one particular individual drew an uncritical, simple house, rapidly drew a tree, spent very little time drawing the human figures, and then spent 20 minutes, drawing in every detail, a 45-automatic revolver with shading and line quality exactness. The careful workmanship on this drawing test, as compared to the previous ones, was very meaningful in terms of overall information. Clinical material obtained by interview indicated an excessive preoccupation with firearms. This individual had not, at the time of his hospitalization, acted out in any way. His preoccupation did, however, become a major area of exploration in his treatment program, revealing well thought out suicidal ideations.

Whenever possible, testing areas should be free of stimuli that may be used in production of Free Drawings. Those that reproduce something seen in the examiner's office (e.g., a book on a desk, a glass of water or coffee nearby) are revealing their resistance to being analyzed. These reproductions can be very telling. For example, one particularly resistant female examinee was tested in a very cluttered office of a hospital where there were innumerable items to copy. Out of this extensive collection of paraphernalia, she chose to draw a picture of the pencil sharpener in the office. The dynamics involved in her being angry, evasive, and castrating were clearly involved in her selection of the pencil sharpener and were confirmed by other psychological measures including observable behavior.

Another example was that of an adult female who drew a picture of a glass that was on the testing desk in the same cluttered office. There was a tremendous amount of information gathered about this subject from earlier projective measures so that her drawing of a glass was extremely significant. In typical hysteric fashion, the examinee had portrayed the glass as an empty vessel, indicating her own needs for external approval for feelings of inner values and self-worth. Historically, she was a chronically angry and dissatisfied woman who was unable to convey these feelings to her husband for fear of his disapproval and rejection.

Since the Free Drawing is created by an individual who has had no structural guidance, the choice, especially if it is unusual, is open to stronger interpretation. As the drawing becomes more and more idiosyncratic in the sense of being unusual, the interpretation is more likely to be accurate. For example, a knife drawn upright would have the expected interpretation of intrapunitive pressures, depression, and possible sexual aggression. This last interpretation becomes even more likely if there are blood drops dripping from the knife. This would be the case of an individual demonstrating uncritical, aggressive ideation. These individuals are usually sadistic psychopaths, who by being so explicit, are telling the examiner that they don't really care what the examiner or society thinks of them or their antisocial behavior.

Individuals with bipolar disorder or mania of all ages tend to overelaborate with less flagrant psychotic qualities, and they sometimes handle their unacceptable anger with humor. For example, one male with bipolar who was experiencing mania asked how much time he had to complete the Free Drawing and was told that he had as much time as he wanted. He then drew an elaborate country scene with a horse and wagon, a farmer with a beard and farmer-type hat in the foreground, farm animals including a donkey, a well, a rake, and many other indications that his drawing was that of a farm. The examiner assessed that he obviously had some point that he was trying to make. When asked what he was drawing, he enthusiastically told the story of the farmer who had gone to town and gotten drunk, come home and stepped on a farm implement, a hoe, and then, he explained, "this man didn't know his ass (the donkey), from the hoe on the ground." Typically, individuals with mania are also more interpersonal and look for interaction that often lets the examiner know, "You are not as intelligent as you think you are, Doc," whereas individuals with schizophrenia and other forms of psychosis are more detached and often draw stars, universe scenes and abstract art when presented with this unstructured Free Drawing test.

Free Drawing Test Interpretations

There are an infinite number of responses to the Free Drawing; however, there are drawings, usual and unusual, that are more commonly seen than others, grouped as follows:

Cars

If you are dealing with a population of male adolescents, especially young males with acting-out and behavior disorder, it is not unusual for them to draw some type of a racecar or ordinary car with indications of speeding. Cars, racecars and speeding cars, are typically a male sexual symbol. It is rare to get a car from a female, even a female with acting-out and behavior-disorder. For a female, this would indicate role disturbance or confusion. One psychologist known to the authors, working in a juvenile detention area, stopped using the Free Drawing because all he kept getting from his homogenous population were racecars. He was unfortunately oblivious to the fact that given the specific, narrow population he was working with and the many common characteristics they shared, the racecar was a common, yet significant response.

Older males, over age 30, who draw cars, raise the question of male aggressiveness in addition to immaturity, especially if the vehicles are drawn moving or speeding (i.e., there are line movements drawn). The older the subject, the more significant the interpretation.

The way a car is drawn is also open to interpretation. The authors have only seen one car drawn with a flat tire, and the interpretation that proved accurate was that of accident-proneness. This drawing was made by a young adolescent male, not yet of driving age, who had had numerous "accidents," including a broken arm and leg in circumstances that were intrapunitive.

An emphasis on the rear portion of the automobile (e.g., a very definite lit taillight, extra detailing of the trunk, a rear end view, etc.) particularly by male subjects, indicates that there is concern with atypical erotic ideation or behavior. It is also significant if a steering wheel is not included in the car drawing, suggesting the incapacity to control aggressive or sexual impulses.

Boats

Boats usually represent a wish to escape and not deal with problem areas. Boats also represent the mother symbol and how the boat sits in the water, if water is drawn, can give some indication of the nurture interaction with the mother figure. The absence of water to support the boat would imply lack of nurturance. The boat's means of propulsion also should be interpreted. If the boat is a sailboat with the drawing of one of its masts going off the top of the page, the typical impotent, passive, castration anxiety interpretation should be considered. If someone is steering the boat, the major aspect to consider is the nurture relationship with the mother symbol.

Airplanes

Airplanes drawn with a frontal view where the propellers resemble a crucifix reflect the aggressive impulses interwoven with the covert schizophrenic processes.

Athletic Fields

Football fields and baseball fields are often obtained, but the interpretation for each is different primarily in that with football fields, especially those with footballs drawn in the air, are usually concretely seen as "I tend to get kicked around." If the Free Drawing is a factual representation of the football field with ten-yard lines drawn across the page, look for distortions or variability in the separation of the lines and for confirmation in the other material of obsessive-compulsive rumination, repetitive ideation or perhaps paranoia and dissatisfaction with thoughts.

Baseball fields do not carry these connotations. With baseball fields, rather than a concrete interpretation, the emphasis is usually a dream or a wish to be successful in sports rather than in school or in a career. The football field may also include this interpretation. Usually, if the Free Drawing is recreational-oriented, the subject is not an academic or professional achiever. Unless the individual is a professional athlete, the interpretation may be, "Work is for other people, I would rather be playing," emphasizing the immature, irresponsible traits of the individual.

Animals

FURRY ANIMALS

Any small, furry, loveable animals are usually obtained from nurture-deprived (real or imagined) individuals who want to be held and coddled. It is not unusual to obtain drawings of furry cats from women. This usually occurs with women who have strong affective needs and expressions (i.e., the hysteric personality). There is also a sensual aspect to a cat as it is soft and fluffy and reflects a more conscious recognition of the need to be stroked, petted and held, taken care of, and pampered. Small dogs or cats drawn by adult males have a similar interpretation to that made for females, plus, the issue of role disturbance or role confusion is likely.

THREATENING ANIMALS

The drawing of a large, aggressive dog (e.g., Rottweiler) is primarily obtained from males with severely aggressive ideation (e.g., sadistic psychopaths).

EXOTIC ANIMALS

The more exotic animals like snakes or lizards also suggest more severe psychopathology. For example, a convicted murder serving a life sentence for cold bloodedly executing seven people took great delight in creating a very unusual and rare Free Drawing of a cobra head with dripping fangs. During the testing, he tried to fake psychosis. The drawing was interpreted as a blatant statement of "I am dangerous, lethal and you had better be careful around me."

COLLARS ON ANIMALS

Accentuated collars, sometimes with spikes or jewels usually give insight into an individual's projections onto their pets. The jeweled collar is usually drawn by hysteric females who need to feel wanted and needed as external reassurances of being valued. The spiked collar is seen in Free Drawings of aggressive, sado-masochistic persons of either gender.

Cartoon Features

Cartoonish features or any sensory mechanism emphasis – visual, auditory (e.g., accentuated eyes or ears), especially when expressed by adolescents or children, whether on the Rorschach, the Human Figure Drawings, or TAT stories, have to be seen as indications of guardedness, paranoid interaction, acute awareness of the environment (although not necessarily schizophrenia), and an assessment of that person's interactions with others. This individual responds very quickly to any nuances or behaviors picked up about the examiner so that while the examiner is testing, the examiner is being tested.

Landscapes and Flowers

Depressed and affectively isolated individuals usually draw landscapes, bouquets, shrubbery, and flowers. These individuals are coping unsuccessfully with feelings of loneliness and being unwanted, usually of a chronic nature.

Flowers usually represent intense affective needs. Males who draw flowers are rare, suggesting affective deprivation and also the possibility of gender confusion or dysphoria. This latter interpretation must consider other circumstances. For example, if the male examinee is a florist, the emphasis of this interpretation must be reduced. The drawing of flowers in this case must also be seen as a retreat to a known, familiar area so as to avoid openly expressing what the unconscious is saying. In attempting to allay the possible passing on of knowledge to the examiner by resorting to something that can always be rationalized as related to the subject's occupation, it may also be suggested that as a florist, the examinee must have accentuated, aesthetic interests.

Landscapes, such as snowcapped mountains, signify a mother seen by the patient as non-nurturing, rejecting, or cold. The feelings of dissatisfaction with obtained nurture usually appear throughout the projective measures.

With seashore scenes, the interpretation depends on whether there are any people drawn, how many, their general ages, whether adults or children, and more importantly, if there is the presence of a sun or a moon in the sky, representing the emphasis of the father or mother (e.g., partial sun, strong rays). For example, large waves on the seashore with an enormous sun symbol in the center of the intersecting mountain peaks is a particular drawing that suggests molestation by a father figure. Of course, such a drawing must be investigated in each case.

Celestial Objects

Historically, the moon has been a symbol of femininity, especially with the menstrual cycle involved, and the interpretation would depend on whether the moon is depicted as full, half, or crescent and the heaviness of the line quality. The sun has invariably involved an expression of father. In one case, a six-year-old who had lost her father in a tragic accident when she was three years old, and who had supposedly dealt with his loss, drew an enormous sun accompanied with the statement, "I like to draw suns." The child should have been in treatment to deal with the loss that she seemed to be handling in superficial functioning.

The Free Drawing of stars in the sky or an astrological chart most frequently comes from individuals with serious ideational defects in primary processes (e.g., individuals with psychosis, schizophrenia, and bipolar disorder).

Religious Symbols

Another common theme in Free Drawings is that of religious symbols. Typically, religious symbols are drawn by individuals with psychosis who have an over-concern with feelings of guilt, right and wrong, and being punished. For example, a 13-year-old drew a picture of Jesus behind a boulder with just the upper portion showing. Religious individuals (e.g., priests, nuns, rabbis) rarely draw religious symbols. The healthier the individual, the less need they have to rely on religious symbolization in Free Drawings and, conversely, the more emphasis on religiosity in the Free Drawing test, the more disturbed the individual.

Abstract Drawings

Free Drawings that resemble abstract art, where the page is a series of curves and darkened areas are sometimes obtained. If something is seen in the abstraction that is significant to the dynamics of the subject, then the drawing should be appreciated. If the drawing simply consists of a series of squiggles with no apparent significance, one must consider resistance. In this case, the subject should be told that the "abstraction is too vague" and should be asked to draw something else. A very intricate, very detailed abstraction; however, is usually an indication of severe ideational disturbance (e.g., schizophrenia).

Other Examples (Less Popular)

BEDS

An adult male drew a Free Drawing of a four-poster bed with fancy, curly cue designs on the headboard. The interpretation was that of concerns with sensual gratification and wellbeing and indications of somatization were found in the shattered line quality of the posts. Additionally, he drew a heavily shaded square at the foot of the bed raising the question of his sexual preference.

Chairs

One of the more common responses of the passive, dependent individual or the individual with identity confusion, particularly males, is a Free Drawing of a chair, or more specifically, a throne-like chair. This also occurs on the Rorschach in response to card 7.

On occasion, an electric chair is drawn, usually as a result of seeing someone in jail under intense environmental stress, and this represents conscious anxiety regarding the possible consequences of the subject's own behavior.

Boxes

One of the characteristics of an individual with strong paranoid schizophrenic disturbances would be seen in the Free Drawing of a box, which symbolizes a place to hide something in (from yourself). An example of this occurred with a cartoonist many years ago. He drew a box with a figure crouched in the corner.

Birthday or holiday gift boxes are extremely rare and generally reflect covert dissatisfaction, particularly in terms of the holiday specified. An example of an unusual birthday gift box was drawn by a male adolescent who drew a darkly blackened box, wrapped with a ribbon and showing an enormous number six (6) on top of the box. As it turned out, the number six represented the age of this individual when trauma had occurred. The blackened gift box was interpreted as "You gave me a gift I didn't want." The gift (trauma) received was that the subject's father had remarried when the subject was six years old.

Monetary Responses

A sheath of bills with a band around the stack indicating that it is a particular sum of money can be seen as an expression of sociopathy and an excessive concern with acquiring money without working for it. "Give me, I deserve this," would be the likely interpretation. It may also represent money received through some type of illicit process. This type of response may also be seen on the Rorschach. For example, a Card VII response to the female figures on the Rorschach were seen as "a check cancelling machine" by a manipulative and psychopathic examinee whose grandmother had control of his finances and was seen as a source of money. This objectification and dehumanization of the grandmother as a check-cashing machine is typical of sociopathic individuals.

Another interpretation may be the individual's lack of motivation for treatment and their dissatisfaction with the fact that the examiner is going to get money rather than the examinee.

A pot of gold at the end of a rainbow is another rare type of monetary response. The rainbow is usually a sign of depression because it looks off into the future with fantasized positive attributes, and, especially with a pot of gold at the end, is usually a fantasy wish for a magical improvement in the subject's life. Rainbows without the pot of gold, although most often received by children, are depressive indicators for both children and adults. Typically, they have given up hope of being "rescued" or "saved" from their difficulties.

Dragons

A fire-breathing dragon with curly cue embellishments or feather-like protrusions would be interpreted in terms of the symbolism represented. For example, the dragon may have a primal scene eye, suggesting severe difficulty with the mother figure. The fire-breathing dragon may also represent disturbed fantasy involving aggression and danger and the flame-like quality of the drawing would raise the question of covert guilt for the examinee's own sexual behavior with the religious implication of "burning in hell." This was obtained from a 20-year-old male whose early years involved divorce and separation from the father and an intense, close, and negative alliance with a mother who exposed him throughout his childhood to Santeria "healers" and repeated "black magic" psychological and physical traumas.

Pencils

Another item often obtained is the drawing of a pencil, which usually indicates resistance, and the direction of the pencil point must be considered in making an interpretation. If the point is directed upwards and is very sharp, the possibility of aggressive and sexual acting out behavior should be considered, especially if the subject is a male adolescent. If the pencil is drawn pointing downward with a more blunted point by a male, the fear of impotence is one likely interpretation of the drawing.

Missing Details

A significant example of missing details on a Free Drawing would be that of a drawing done by a young man who had in actuality committed suicide some months following his psychiatric hospitalization. He drew a sun with eyes and a mouth but no nose, looking down at a petaled flower with a face, also drawn without a nose. The drawing suggested that the father was not accepting of the passive, depressed, dysfunctional son. The petaled, noseless flower suggests that, in spite of his anger, he was similar in personality structure to the father in terms of non-achievement and role disturbances indicated in the missing nose portion of each face. The eyes were handled in terms of single line slashes, and the mouth was drawn in an upward single line, as though smiling. While both were smiling, he included in the picture what appears to be a rain cloud, strongly suggesting covert depression indicators. In addition, there was an unusual, heavy fence drawn behind the flower, and this suggests that in spite of his "smiling" confidence, he was a very angry and dissatisfied individual, which was sadly confirmed by his suicide.

Free Drawing Scores:

48 Knives

All: Verbal, physical, and sexual aggression, particularly if there are blood drops dripping from the knife. This would reflect an individual, usually a sadistic psychopath, expressing uncritical, sadistic, and threateningly aggressive ideation. They do not care what the examiner or society thinks of them or their antisocial behavior.

49 Overelaborate drawing (e.g., a barnyard scene with horse, wagon, barn, rake)

All: Bi-polar mania

50 Cars, trucks, vans, or racing cars

Males:

Movement and acting out, behavior disorder tendencies.

Figure 6.1 Drawn by a 14-year-old male two years after his father's accidental death, the acting out tendencies suggested by a moving vehicle are consistent with his history of subsequent fighting at school and other test data suggestive of impulsivity, anger, and proneness to aggression.

50a *Females:*

Possible gender confusion or dysphoria

50b *Individuals over age 40:*

Often aggressive and immature

50c Vehicles with a flat tire

All: Suggest accident proneness

50d Vehicles with rear taillights that are accentuated (in size and/or attention to detail), rear-end views or extra detailing of rear portion, or any drawing of a train

All: Atypical erotic ideation or behavior

51 Boats, regardless of the geographic location of the assessment

All: Usually represent dependency features and a wish to escape from and avoid responsibilities

51a The absence of water to support the boat or drawing the boat suspended above the water line

All: Lack of nurture and ongoing pursuit of nurture, particularly in terms of mother/female figures; consider chemical dependency.

51b A sailboat with a mast extending off the top of the page

Males:
Suggests emasculation anxiety

Females:
No interpretation

51c The omission of someone steering the boat (any boat)

All: Poor impulse control, a lack of self-criticalness, and limited insight into his or her behavior

52 Any vehicle extending off of the page

All: Poor judgment, poor planning, and acting out aggression

53 Football fields with ten-yard markers

All: Obsessive-compulsive ruminations, repetitive ideation, passive-aggressive tendencies, paranoia, and dissatisfaction with conscious ideations.

53a *Females:*

Gender confusion or dysphoria

54 Baseball fields

All: A regressive fantasy, a dream or wish to return to a responsibility-free era in childhood; the narcissistic and grandiose aspects also suggest a lack of self-confidence and a manipulative method of obtaining success

55 Furry animals (i.e., animals that have fur, regardless of whether the fur is drawn)

All: Strong unmet affective needs. The individual desires to be held, caressed (in a pre-pubescent, non-sexual manner). Protection from harm and responsibility are paramount.

Adults only:

Dependency and immaturity

Figure 6.2 This cat was drawn by a 12-year-old girl who, along with her parents, was in a car accident resulting in traumatic brain injury and persistent increased clinginess with her parents, fear of something bad happening to them, and nightmares of such. Drawing of a furry animal suggests consideration of unmet affective needs, acknowledging the girl's need for affection and nurture was likely heightened due to trauma.

56   Threatening animals (e.g., large, aggressive dogs, a Cobra's head, a wolf, etc. Animals that are aggressive or frightening to most people, including fictional animals in a threatening pose)

All: Severe aggressive, dangerous ideation and actions

57   Jewelry of all types

All: Self-dissatisfaction and a need to obtain external reassurances of being valued; consider depression, histrionic personality, borderline personality, and anti-social personality.

58   Cartoon figures

All: Guardedness, immaturity, and acute awareness of and mistrust of the environment

59   Landscapes

All: Usually drawn by depressed individuals who are feeling lonely and unwanted; landscapes are suggestive of mother/child relationships, and, depending on the details, suggest the mother as giving and nurturing or rejecting and cold.

60   Flowers

All: Intense affective needs.

60a *Males:*

Affective deprivation and gender confusion or dysphoria

61   Celestial Objects

All: Usually drawn by individuals with severe reality/fantasy deficits (i.e., poor reality testing).

61a Stars in the sky or an astrological chart

All: Consider psychoses and schizoaffective disorders.

61b The moon

All: Reflects a symbol of femininity in terms of the menstrual cycle, thus a moon drawing suggests ongoing conflicts with mother, particularly if the moon is half or less.

61c The sun

All: Suggests a strong and unresolved attachment to father, particularly when the sun is large or has rays extending outward.

62 Religious symbols

All: Typically drawn by individuals with psychosis who have illogical preoccupations with guilt, right, and wrong. Religious figures rarely draw religious symbols. The healthier the individual, the less they need to rely on external religiosity.

63 Abstract drawings like abstract art (i.e., content is vague or unrecognizable)

All: Usually reflects manipulation, guardedness, and resistance, particularly if drawn quickly and non-critically.

63a Intricate, compulsively detailed abstraction

All: Severe ideational disturbance

64 Bed(s)

All: Sensual concerns and tendencies toward somatization and manipulation through somatic complaints

65 Chair(s)

All: Passivity, dependency, and passive-aggressive tendencies

65a An electric chair

All: Intense environmental stress regarding possible consequences of the individual's behavior

65b A throne

All: Feelings of inferiority manifested by stereotypic, pseudo-masculine compensatory behavior

66 Box(es)

All: Rare and reflect paranoid and paranoid schizophrenic disturbances. The box symbolizes a place to hide something, usually from oneself.

67 Monetary symbols (e.g., a sheath of bills wrapped with a band around the stack, paper money, coins, dollar and cent symbols)

All: Often reflect sociopathy and an excessive concern with money without working for it; The narcissistic sociopathic individual's view of, "give me this, I deserve it" is probable. Monetary symbols are suggestive of low motivation for treatment, poor insight and depression (i.e., The hopelessness in, "I must steal or win the lottery because I cannot earn it appropriately.")

68   A pot of gold at the end of the rainbow

All: Another monetary response; it suggests depression, with the fantasy of a magical solution to the individual's lifelong problems.

69   Dragon(s)

All: Excessive fantasy often involving aggression and anger; substance abuse is often associated with dragon drawings.

69a Flames or flame-like features

All: Covert guilt for the individual's real or fantasized sexual behavior, for which he or she will "burn in hell."

70   Pencil(s)

All: Guardedness and resistance

70a Pencil pointed upward

All: Sexual aggressivity

70b Pencil pointed downward

All: Impotence

71   Vases with or without flowers

All: Self-dissatisfaction, narcissism, and nurture depletion, (i.e., empty-vessel syndrome)

7 Advanced Scoring System for the Bender Gestalt Test – Revised (ABGT-R)

The Advanced Scoring System for the Bender Gestalt Test-Revised (ABGT-R) (Raphael et al., 2012) is a reliable and empirically validated projective test that has been found to have predictive power in evaluating personality and neuropsychological functioning. The ABGT-R has been empirically correlated with the MMPI and MMPI-2 (Raphael & Golden, 2002). The 207-item scoring system is an enhancement of the original Advanced Psychodiagnostic Interpretation (API) (Reichenberg, N., & Raphael, A. J., 1992) 112-item system and includes additional indicators of psychologic and personality pathology and neurological deficits. Like its predecessor, the ABGT-R measures indicators of depression, anxiety, psychosis, dangerousness, impulsivity, addiction-proneness, trauma, intellectual disability, and neurocognitive disorder in the reproduction of BGT drawings. Readers are referred to Drs. Reichenberg and Raphael (1992) and Raphael et al. (2012) for discussion of the developmental research on the API.

A 1997 study by Raphael and Golden (Raphael et al., 2012) found that a brief projective test battery, including the ABGT-R, HTP, and Free Drawing, was useful in predicting 6-month job retention rates in correctional officers at a statistically significant level. As in the current text, the authors sought support for the use of a brief and easily administered battery that is economical and culturally fair.

Several published studies have reported on the psychometric properties of the ABGT-R. Results of inter-rater reliability testing suggested that raters can easily and quickly learn the 207-item scoring system and produce high rates of agreement. After a 90-minute training, nine raters scored three BGT protocols and demonstrated 100% on 156 of the 207 items, with an average of 94% specific item agreement between raters, which ranged from 56% to 100% across items. The overall agreement on the three protocols ranged from 93% to 95% (Aucone et al., 1999). The ABGT-R was found to have satisfactory test-retest reliability when administered to outpatients diagnosed with schizophrenia twice with a mean interval of 6.4 years between administrations. After completing a 90-minute training in the system, five doctoral students and two Master's level students in counseling

DOI: 10.4324/9781003308799-7

psychology scored 80 BGT protocols. The mean reliability was .74 and ranged from .71 to .80. Lending further support to previous inter-rater reliability testing, raters demonstrated an average of 85.97% agreement, ranging from 79% to 97% (Aucone et al., 2001).

The ABGT-R was correlated to the MMPI in the first study ever to examine interrelationships between these two measures, and the authors found no other studies at that time examining relationships between the MMPI and other respected personality measures (Raphael & Golden, 2002). The ABGT-R and MMPI protocols of 279 adult outpatients were analyzed. Of the 207 ABGT-R items that did not include gender-specific distortions or that occurred with a frequency of less than 15%, 55 items remained and were factor analyzed to produce 17 factors. The factors included Trauma and Stress; Anxiety and Dependency; Aggressivity and Impulse Control; Conversion Hysteria and Depression; Cognitive Impairment; Anxiety and Denial of Mistrust; Social Introversion, Impulsivity; Anxiety; Dissociation; Schizotypal; Antisocial; Borderline; Anger; Hypochondriasis; Schizophrenia; Addiction-prone; Hypomania; Dependency; Depressed; Low Self-Esteem; Intrapunative Depression; Antisocial Functioning; Isolation and Paranoia; Authority Conflict; and Psychasthenia and Psychopathic Deviate. First-order calculations between MMPI variables and ABGT-R factors generated significant correlations for 13 of the ABGT-R factors. To assess the ability of the ABGT-R to predict each mean MMPI scale score, multiple regressions were conducted to correlate the 12 MMPI scales with the 17 ABGT-R factors, and ten of the 12 MMPI scales were found to have significant correlations. These correlations ranged from .36 to .47, with eight of the ten being significant at the .01 level or better and the remaining two significant at the .05 level. Discriminant analysis was conducted to classify protocols into high and low pathology groups. Of the 279 subjects, 76% were accurately classified, with 25 of the 93 low pathology subjects and 18 of the 91 high pathology subjects being misclassified. This clear relationship between the MMPI and ABGT-R is particularly important in that the ABGT-R is less susceptible to fatigue and motivation than the MMPI and does not have the limitations of cultural bias and influence of reading ability. While it is certainly not a substitute for the MMPI, the ABGT-R is a valuable adjunct to a battery including the MMPI. In cases in which time constraints, resources, or examinee factors preclude the use of the MMPI, the ABGT-R can be used to answer clinical questions about the same or similar matters.

8 Case Examples

This chapter contains several case examples, including more contextual information than what is provided in captions throughout the preceding chapters. Please note that some identifying information has been changed or omitted to protect the confidentiality of the person to whom it pertains.

Case #1

Miss X was a 16-year-old female who was an inpatient at the time of evaluation due to cocaine abuse, which she identified as a problem. She also reported academic difficulty. Her human figure drawings were significant for dark lines, indicating anger and hostility, and clothing pockets, suggesting exaggerated dependency. Perhaps more significant, the dark shading was focused on the pants pockets, in which the figures hands were concealed, though poorly, as the arm lines were still visible and not adequately erased or shaded over. Her drawings had indications of impulse control problems, particularly related to expressing anger. Her drawings were also suggestive of a history of trauma, and her female figure drawing indicated possible primal scene trauma.

Perhaps the most telling was her free drawing of a downward pointing pencil, which she labeled, "Pencil," an indication of her feelings of impotence in overcoming her substance abuse and being able to function outside of the hospital setting. When prompted to produce a free drawing that was not a likeness of something in the room (i.e., the pencil), she drew two flowers with a grass underline, suggesting intense affective needs. The findings from the drawing tests, particularly indications of impulsiveness, dependency, and trauma, were supported by her MMPI profile, Sentence Completion Test, Rorschach, and Bender Gestalt Test. She did not know her father, due to her parents' separation when she was one year old, and many of her Sentence Completion responses lamented this traumatic loss. Her MMPI profile represented a "cry for help" and impulsivity, despite her façade of normal functioning and nonchalance toward her problems. Consistent with her drawing tests, her Rorschach and BGT were laden with indications of libidinal turmoil (Figures 8.1–8.8).

DOI: 10.4324/9781003308799-8

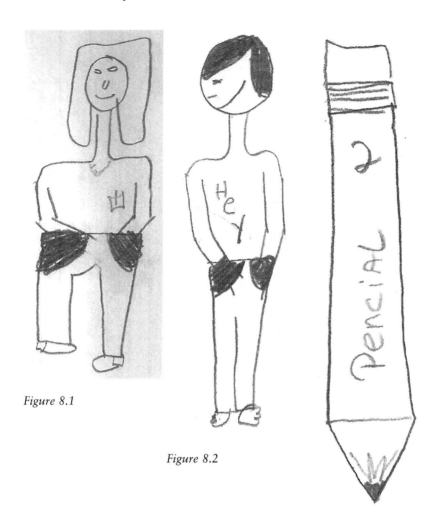

Figure 8.1

Figure 8.2

Figure 8.3

Case #2

Miss Y was a 30-year-old female presenting for psychological evaluation for diagnostic clarification and treatment recommendations. She reported a history of multiple traumas, ongoing depression and difficulty regulating her mood, self-injurious behaviors, and chronic marijuana use since adolescence. She described resentment and jealousy of the attention given to her siblings by her parents. She reported being a victim of bullying, sexual exploitation and assault, and domestic violence. She had difficulty keeping friends due to jealousy and difficulty maintaining employment due to conflicts with supervisors. She lived alone, had never been married, and had no children.

Miss Y's two-dimensional house drawing was suggestive of regression, resistance, and guardedness in exposing internal conflicts and ideation. Also suggestive of resistance and circumspect behavior or severely limited intellectual capabilities, the house was scorable as a "face" house. [Given the claimant's history of attaining a Master's degree without special education or support, severely limited intellectual capabilities can be ruled out.] The windows reflecting multiple stories in the house drawing suggests limited ability to maintain goal-directed behavior and that she may be irresponsible, immature, ineffectual, and rely on the competence of their partners or families. Miss Y's use of the bottom edge of the paper as the foundation is suggestive of extreme anxiety and insecurity. Impulse control problems are indicated by the cross-hatched windows. Overall, the scorable features of Miss Y's face house suggested traits consistent with her history including irresponsibility and resistance to maturing evidenced in her daily marijuana use, ongoing jealousy of her siblings and resentment toward her parents, as well as conflict with authority figures and inability to keep a job (with associated reliance on her family of origin for financial support).

Miss Y's tree drawing, like her house drawing, also utilized the bottom of the page as a base. While this would be developmentally normative for a child, it suggests insecurity and dependency on external support. The heavy shading and dark lines are indicative of depression, consistent with her complaints and findings from other personality measures (both objective and projective). Also consistent with her reported history were suggestions of extreme anger and violence proneness indicated by drawing a "spiked" tree on which the top part of the tree is depicted in numerous straight lines in upward projections. The most prominent feature of the tree is a darkly lined hole encompassing the entire width (and much of the length) of the trunk, suggestive of trauma.

Note the convergence of findings between Miss Y's house and tree drawing, both of which suggest insecurity and dependency. They also yield a combination of impulsivity, anger, and violence proneness between the two drawings that is consistent with Miss Y's report of anger and aggressive behavior since early adolescence, as well as experiencing "heightened situations" in which she feels "enraged, angry, hysterical, and trapped." Observations of her behavior during testing revealed her affect varied among negative mood states, including anger, sadness, and calm.

Miss Y's approach to person drawings was remarkable for drawing a male figure first. While this could suggest gender confusion, historical context and her responses to the inquiry phase also raise hypotheses regarding identification with males. Upon inquiry, Miss Y indicated that the drawing was an 18-year-old high school student who "just likes to smoke weed." Note the male figure is drawn with a smile. The second drawing, however, depicts two female figures – one alive and one dead. The talon-like fingers are suggestive of aggression, wrist lines suggestive of self-harm, and dark lines suggestive of anger and hostility. Again, note the convergence of findings across drawings and other sources of assessment data.

Finally, Miss Y's family drawing is telling at first glance. She has drawn a line between herself and the rest of her family members. She has drawn her family of origin, reflecting her frustrated dependency needs and perhaps because she had not yet developed the psychological maturity to maintain a relationship with a significant other. She drew herself first, followed by her youngest sibling, mother, brother seated at the head of the table, and her father. She has drawn herself with a frown, dad and youngest sibling with neutral expressions, and mother and brother with smiles. She discussed that her brother is happy because he always gets what he wants, mom is naive, and I'm over here alone and depressed … " The distance and line drawn between her and other family members reflects feelings of rejection. Both siblings are drawn larger than Miss Y and their parents, indicating a lack of adequate limit-setting by parents. This, too, was consistent with her perception of family dynamics in which one brother was described as "the boss" due to his mental illness, antisocial personality traits, and use of scare tactics and violence. The other sibling was an adult but had a developmental disorder and not capable of independent living.

Figure 8.4

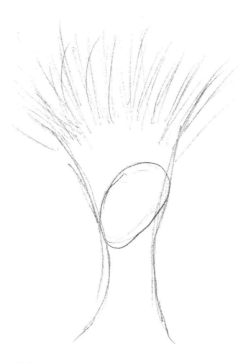

Figure 8.5

Figure 8.6

Figure 8.7

Figure 8.8

9 Research on the Cross-Cultural Psychological Assessment Battery: The Raphael Methodology (CCPAB)

Inter-Rater Reliability of the Raphael Projective System (RPS) of Scoring Projective Drawings

The authors examined the inter-rater reliability of the CCPAB, which was referred to as the Raphael Projective System (RPS) at the time. The study found good agreement among raters. In sum, one of the authors provided training on the scoring system for approximately one hour to five graduate students in a clinical psychology doctoral program. Immediately following the training, the students independently scored ten house drawing tests, ten tree drawing tests, and ten person drawing tests using the newly learned scoring system. The students' ratings were then compared to the correct ratings as determined by consensus of the first three authors. Examination of the students' percentage of agreement with the authors found agreement ranging from 89.6% to 92.1% (average of 90.90% for all five students) on the house drawings. The students demonstrated 83.3% to 88.5% agreement with the authors (average of 86.48% agreement for all five students) on tree drawings. The student demonstrated 82.5% to 88.9% agreement with the authors (average of 85.43% agreement for all five students) on person drawings. Please find below the entire study as published.

Introduction

Delineating details on any protective measure is very much like describing snowflakes in that all are basically unique. Any oddity of inclusion or omission and any distortion should be considered for interpretation by the examiner. It is extremely difficult to describe each specific response obtained and its corresponding interpretation. Variables such as age, ethnicity, gender, physical status, education, and reason for evaluation must be considered in the accurate scoring and interpretation of all psychological measures. There are ever-increasing demands placed on the social sciences to create better, quicker, more

DOI: 10.4324/9781003308799-9

accurate, and less expensive methods of assessing what is real about an individual in traits such as honesty, fitness for duty, competence, dangerousness, self-control, and more.

The seemingly infinite nature of potential responses to projective drawing prompts has made it difficult to standardize an interpretive system. This has contributed to reluctance among practitioners to use these time-honored methods amidst the current emphasis on objective and quantitative assessment measures. The Raphael Projective System (RPS) is an approach to administering and scoring projective drawings, including the Bender Gestalt Test, House-Tree-Person drawings, Kinetic Family Drawings, and Free Drawings, that aims to improve reliability and accuracy in interpretation of results. A comprehensive manual for the administration, scoring, and interpretation of projective drawings using the RPS approach is in development. In anticipation of its completion, the authors conducted this investigation into the IRR of the scoring system.

Method

Ratings

Dr. Raphael, Dr. Ascheman, and Dr. Miller expounded and refined Drs. Reichenberg and Raphael's preliminary system for scoring projective drawings. Through numerous and lengthy discussions, scoring criteria were clarified to reduce subjectivity in determination of binary scoring (i.e., a score of 1 = *present* or *yes* and 0 = *absent* or *no*. Such clarifications included changing relative terms of criteria such as "close" or "disproportionate" to specific units of measurement such as "within a quarter of an inch" or "more than one third of the overall size." The scoring criteria underwent several iterations before the authors determined that subjectivity within each item had been sufficiently minimized or eliminated such that the resultant criteria could easily be taught to psychological assessment practitioners with varying levels of experience, including trainees, and uniformly applied to the interpretation of drawings from clients as young as age eight years. The number of criteria for each category of drawings varied, and are as follows: House drawings = 55, Tree drawings = 33, and Person drawings = 25.

Materials and Participants

Next, drawings were selected from a sample derived from an outpatient private practice in a metropolitan area (Miami, Florida) that had been collected over a 30-year period. Dr. Ascheman chose ten House drawings, ten Tree drawings, and ten Person drawings that were observed to contain many of the scoring criteria. Drs. Raphael, Ascheman, and Miller met to independently score each drawing and then jointly reviewed their responses until consensus was achieved regarding the correct score. Dr. Raphael then provided training on the scoring system for approximately one hour to five graduate students in a clinical psychology doctoral program with assistance from Dr. Ascheman.

Procedure

Immediately following the training, the students independently scored the same ten House drawing tests, ten Tree drawing tests, and ten Person drawing tests using the newly learned scoring system. The students' ratings were then compared to the correct ratings as determined by consensus. The number of correct scores was counted for each drawing scored by each rater. The correct scores were summed for each rater on each category of drawings (i.e., House, Tree, and Person), and total percentages correct were calculated for raters on each category. The percentages correct were averaged for the five raters for each category of drawing. The number of correct responses for each category and student rater can be found in Appendix A.

Since percentages of agreement do not correct for agreements that would be expected by chance, an inter-rater reliability (IRR) analysis was performed to assess the degree that the five student raters consistently assigned the correct binary ratings (*present/absent*) to each of the 1,130 items (ten House drawings × 55 items, + ten Tree drawings × 33 items, + ten Person drawings × 25 items). Based on our data, Cohen's (unweighted) kappa (Cohen, 1960) was deemed an appropriate index of IRR. Kappa was therefore computed for each rater's individual item scores paired with the correct scores (as agreed upon by the authors prior to the study), then averaged to provide a single index of IRR (Conger, 1980).

We were also interested to examine how consistent the students' and authors' scores were with each other, and computed kappa for each coder pair (both students and authors) with an averaged single index.

Results

Inter-Rater Agreement

Examination of the students' percentage of agreement with the authors found agreement ranging from 91.6% to 94.2% (average of 93.1% for all five students) on the House drawings. The students demonstrated 82.1% to 87.9% agreement with the authors (average of 85.4% agreement for all five students) on Tree drawings, and 83.6% to 91.2% agreement with the authors (average of 87.8% agreement for all five students) on Person drawings. The specific percentages for each rater and category of drawings are displayed below in Table 9.1.

Table 9.1 Percentages Correct by Student Raters

Drawing	Rater 1	Rater 2	Rater 3	Rater 4	Rater 5	Average
House	94.2	91.6	94.0	94.2	91.8	93.2
Tree	85.5	82.1	87.9	85.2	86.4	85.4
Person	91.2	89.6	87.2	83.6	86.4	87.8
All Drawings	90.9	88.5	90.7	89.3	89.2	89.7

Inter-Rater Reliability (IRR)

In calculating the IRR, the marginal distributions of our binary ratings showed a substantially greater number of *absent* or *no* ratings, indicating a prevalence problem. The difference between the probability of *yes* and the probability of *no* is the Prevalence Index (PI). When *yes* and *no* are equally probable, the PI = 0, which gives more reliable kappa values (PI's are presented in Table 9.2). If the PI is high, then kappa is reduced accordingly (Cicchetti & Feinstein, 1990). Therefore, an adjusted kappa statistic for skewed prevalence (PABAK) was used to determine a more accurate level of agreement (Byrt, Bishop, & Carlin, 1993). Although PABAK has received some criticism in the literature, there seems to be agreement that kappa values can be considered reliable when good agreement is obtained despite skewed prevalence. In the Table 9.2 below, we listed our original Cohen's kappa statistics, the adjusted kappa, and the prevalence rates, in order to highlight the prevalence effect and allow a clearer interpretation of results than would have been available with a single index of agreement.

The resulting kappa values for each student rater's agreement with the authors' consensus (as indicated in the table below) indicate excellent agreement on House drawings, $k = .864$, Tree drawings, $k = .710$, and Person drawings $k = .764$, with a substantial average kappa for all drawings, $k = .779$.

We then compared the level of agreement between each student and author with each of the other students and authors. As depicted in Addendum B, there was excellent agreement between most pairs of raters (students and the authors) with an overall average kappa of $k = .79$.

Indices of Positive and Negative Agreement

Approximately only 20% of all items were scored *yes* in the drawings. With such a relatively small amount of positive ratings, we were interested in the probability that any two randomly assigned raters would both assign a *yes* rating. We calculated Cicchetti and Feinstein's (1990) indices of positive and negative agreement ($p_{pos} = 2a/[N + a - d]$ and $p_{neg} = 2d/[N - a + d]$), as we felt separate indices of agreement for

Table 9.2 Inter-Rater Reliability (Student Raters × Consensus)

Rater/Drawing	Kappa	Adjusted Kappa	CI*	Prevalence** Index
Rater 1				
House	.81	.88		.63
Tree	.59	.71		.55
Person	.77	.86		.45
Rater 1 All Drawings	.73	.82	.80–.84	.57
Rater 2				
House	.72	.84		.64
Tree	.52	.64		.51
Person	.75	.80		.44
Rater 2 All Drawings	.67	.77	.75–.79	.56
Rater 3				
House	.80	.88	.	.64
Tree	.64	.76		.57
Person	.66	.74		.51
Rater 3 All Drawings	.72	.81	79–.83	.59
Rater 4				
House	.81	.88		.63
Tree	.57	.71		.57
Person	.61	.68		.43
Rater 4 All Drawings	.69	.79	.77–.81	.57
Rater 5				
House	.73	.84		.63
Tree	.59	.73		.59
Person	.68	.74		.46
Rater 5 All Drawings	.68	.78	.76–.80	.58
House Drawings Average	.77	.86	—	.63
Tree Drawings Average	.58	.71	—	.59
Person Drawings Average	.69	.76	—	.46
All Drawings	.70	.80	—	.57

Note: * CI: Confidence Interval 95%; Prevalence Index = Difference between probability of "yes" and probability of "no."

positively and negatively scored items would contribute to providing more transparency to our results (see Table 9.3 below for results). The results show that it is extremely likely (>90%) that if one rater were to assign a positive rating, a second rater would also rate a *yes*.

Discussion

These authors are encouraged by the results, which suggest strong IRR among even novice assessment practitioners. These statistics are comparable to that of other studies examining the reliability of scoring

Table 9.3 Indices of Student Raters' Positive and Negative Agreement with
        Consensus Scores

	Rater 1	Rater 2	Rater 3	Rater 4	Rater 5
Positive Agreement	.94	.93	.94	.93	.93
Negative Agreement	.79	.74	.77	.75	.74

methods for projective drawings. For example, Van Hutton (1994) tested the IRR of her system by comparing consistency between two clinicians' scoring of the House-Tree-Person drawings of 20 children. After revisions of several items, the raters were in agreement 93.2% of the time, and each scoring item met the cutoff criteria of being consistently rated 80% of the time on the drawings of ten additional child subjects. Similarly, inter-rater studies of the Advanced Scoring System for the Bender Gestalt Test-Revised (ABGT-R) (Raphael, Golden, & Raphael, 2012) also yielded results suggesting that raters can easily and quickly learn the 207-item scoring system and produce high rates of agreement. After a 90-minute training, nine raters scored three BGT protocols and demonstrated 100% agreement on 156 of the 207 items, with an average of 94% specific item agreement between raters, which ranged from 56% to 100% across items. The overall agreement on the three protocols ranged from 93% to 95% (Aucone et al., 1999). Moreover, the ABGT-R was found to have satisfactory test-retest reliability when administered to outpatients diagnosed with schizophrenia twice with a mean interval of 6.4 years between administrations. After completing a 90-minute training on the system, five doctoral students and two Master's level students in counseling psychology scored 80 BGT protocols. The mean reliability was .74 and ranged from .71 to .80. Lending further support to previous IRR testing, raters demonstrated an average of 85.97% agreement, ranging from 79% to 97% (Aucone et al., 2001).

While this study found adequate reliability of the RPS scoring system, the results have not yet been replicated. Upon release of the RPS manual, including scoring criteria, the authors encourage other assessment practitioners and researchers to learn, utilize, and further study the method. It will be especially important to investigate the reliability of the method among practitioners who were not trained by its developer.

Furthermore, additional inquiries of research may include correlating the RPS interpretive results with results from other measures. Past results by other researchers on relationships between projective and objective measures have been mixed in this regard. For example, Gillespie (1994) promoted validation by advising examiners to compare results of Mother-and-Child drawings with MMPI profiles; however, the author did not provide empirical analysis of statistical relationships between the drawing test and the objective MMPI, which could have provided more support for the validity of drawing tests. In contrast, the ABGT-R has been empirically validated to have predictive power in evaluating personality and neuropsychological functioning. The ABGT-R has been empirically correlated with the MMPI and MMPI-2 (Raphael & Golden, 2002). Future studies investigating the correlation between projective and objective methods will continue to shed light on the utility of projective methods for answering clinical and forensic assessment questions.

References

Aucone, E. J., Raphael, A. J., Golden, C. J., Espe-Pfeifer, P., Seldon, J., Pospisil, T., Dornheim, L., Proctor-Weber, Z., & Calabria, M. (1999). Reliability of the Advanced Psychodiagnostic Interpretation (API) scoring system for the Bender Gestalt. *Assessment, 68*(3), 301–303.

Aucone, E. J., Wagner, E. E., Raphael, A. J., Golden, C. J., Espe-Pfeifer, P., Dornheim, L., Seldon, J., Pospisil, T., Proctor-Weber, Z., & Calabria, M. (2001). Test-retest reliability of the Advanced Psychodiagnostic Interpretation (API) scoring system for the Bender Gestalt in chronic schizophrenics. *Assessment, 8*(3), 351–353.

Byrt, T., Bishop, J. & Carlin, J. (1993). Bias, prevalence and kappa. *Journal of Clinical Epidemiology, 46*, 423–429.

Cicchetti, D. V., & Feinstein, A. R. (1990) High agreement but low kappa II: Resolving the paradoxes. *Journal of Clinical Epidemiology, 43*, 551–558.

Cohen J. (1960). A coefficient of agreement for nominal scales. *Educational and Psychological Measurement, 20*(1), 37–46.

Conger, A. J. (1980). Integration and generalization of kappas for multiple raters. *Psychological Bulletin, 88*(2), 322–328.

Gillespie, J. (1994). *The Projective use of Mother-and-Child Drawings: A Manual for Clinicians.* New York: Brunner/Mazel, Inc.

Landis, J. R., & Koch, G. G. (1977). The measurement of observer agreement for categorical data. *Biometrics, March, 33*(1), 159–174.

McHugh, M. L. (2012). Interrater reliability: The kappa statistic. *Biochemia Medica, 22*(3), 276–282.

Raphael, A. J., & Golden, C. J. (2002). Relationships of objectively scored Bender variables with MMPI scores in an outpatient psychiatric population. *Perceptual and Motor Skills, 95*(3), 1217–1232.

Raphael, A. J., Golden, C., & Raphael, M. A. (2012). *The Advanced Scoring System for the Bender Gestalt Test- Revised (ABGT-R): Ages 8–80.* Deer Park, NY: Linus Publications, Inc.

Van Hutton, V. (1994). *House-Tree-Person and Draw-A-Person as measures of abuse in children: A quantitative scoring system.* Odessa, FL: Psychological Assessment Resources, Inc.

10 Summary and Conclusions

Areas of Future Research

The book would be up-to-date indefinitely pending further research. The methodology that underlies the battery has been researched for decades and research is ongoing. The methods described in the book continued to be the relied upon methods for administration, while the scoring and interpretation of the tests continued to be validated through continued study.

Furthermore, additional inquiries of research may include correlating the CCPAM interpretive results with results from other measures. Past results by other researchers on relationships between projective and objective measures have been mixed in this regard. For example, Gillespie (1994) promoted validation by advising examiners to compare results of Mother-and-Child drawings with MMPI profiles; however, the author did not provide empirical analysis of statistical relationship between the drawing test and the objective MMPI, which could have provided more support for the validity of drawing tests. In contrast, the ABGT-R has been empirically validated to have predictive power in evaluating personality and neuropsychological functioning. The ABGT-R has been empirically correlated with the MMPI and MMPI-2 (Raphael & Golden, 2002). Future studies investigating the correlation between projective and objective methods will continue to shed light on the utility of projective methods for answering clinical and forensic assessment questions.

Limitations

While the reliability of the CCPAM scoring system has been established in one study, the results have not yet been replicated. Upon release of this CCPAM manual, including scoring criteria, the authors encourage other assessment practitioners and researchers to learn, utilize, and further study the method. It will be especially important to investigate the reliability of the method among practitioners who were not trained by its developer.

DOI: 10.4324/9781003308799-10

It also will be important to continue the validation process of the CCPAM. It has not yet been cross validated with other measures of psychological functioning, either objective or projective. Such studies will be important to affirm its clinical utility. Moreover, validating the CCPAM for assessment of specific constructs, such as trauma or depression, has not yet been established.

Benefits

The book provides a step-by-step, user-friendly manual that will provide a brief personality assessment battery including projective methods. The manual is appropriate for users ranging from graduate-level students in training and supervision to even the most skilled assessment psychologists for quick and valid assessment of a wide range of clients. This method is particularly relevant among the current psychological assessment climate of emphasizing the selection of culturally fair and reliable tools for obtaining valid results. As this method does not solely rely on language to convey personality information, any person with the requisite motor skills to hold a pencil is a good candidate use. Furthermore, this method has been validated to accurately assess aspects of personality functioning that may or may not be revealed upon self-report personality testing.

Appendix A

Scoring Key for HTP, KFD, and Free Drawings

House Drawing Test (#1–32): The house test reflects the status of interpersonal relationships, maturation, and movement towards adulthood regardless of the age of the subject.

#	Feature	Indicated	Interpretation
1	Two dimensional houses by adults		Regression, resistance and guardedness in exposing interpersonal conflicts or disturbed ideation.
2	Face house-rectangular box (face), windows (eyes), door (mouth) and triangle roof (hair) drawn by adults		Resistance, circumspect behavior, or severely limited intellectual capabilities.
3	Windows reflecting multiple stories		Tendencies towards pseudo-striving and the limited ability of the individual to maintain goal-directed behavior. These individuals are often irresponsible, immature, and ineffectual and reply on the competence of their partners or families.
4	Children (ages 6 to 18) who place the house at the bottom (on the edge) of the page		Emphasizes appropriate developmental security needs.
	Adults who use the bottom of the page (on the edge) as the base or foundation for their house drawing		Extremely anxious, insecure individuals.

(Continued)

#	Feature	Indicated	Interpretation
5	When a portion of the house does not fit on the page and is omitted		Questions are: which rooms were cut off or omitted should be asked. Omitted kitchens point to dependency features; bedrooms omitted point to sexual concerns; living rooms omitted point to peer relationship conflicts.
6	Aerial view houses		Reflect extreme caution and mistrust in interpersonal relationships and is typical of psychosis, paranoia, and individuals with profound gender identification disturbances. Poor self-concepts hidden by detachment and isolation are suggested.
7	Floor plan houses		Typical of severely isolated, paranoid and psychotic teenagers and adults. The pathology is usually more severe with floor plan homes than with aerial view homes. Individuals with regressive depression, paranoid schizophrenia, and schizoaffective disorder often draw floor plan houses.
8	Young children (ages 6–12) who draw houses that take up 2/3 or more of the page in height, and are three inches or more in width, with emphasized chimneys (e.g., disproportionately larger or darkened, or attention to detail such as with brick work)		Reflects the limited social areas open to the child.
9	Chimneys slanted ≥45° from vertical		Normal for young children. Adolescents and adults who draw slanted chimneys often are regressed and immature in their social functioning.

(Continued)

#	Feature	Indicated	Interpretation
10	Chimneys with smoke emerging		Important indicators of impulse control capabilities. Indicate impulsive expression of anger. The darker the line quality of the smoke, the more intense the anger and the weaker the controls on the expression of the anger.
11	The number of chimneys drawn		Indicates the degree of conscious concern related to impulse control. More than one chimney would suggest intense anxiety over loss of control and a psychotic preoccupation with control of unacceptable impulses.
12	Specific architectural style (e.g., log cabins, igloos, etc.)		Reflects the individual's residence or prior residence. *The scoring occurs if the subject has no experience in the type of house drawn.* An **igloo** house is extremely rare and suggests frigid, obsessive-compulsive, anhedonic traits. **Tree houses** are also very rare and reflect immaturity, isolation, eccentricity, peer disturbance, and a desire to return to a less responsible time in the individual's life. The older the individual the greater the likelihood of regressive functioning.
13	Houses that take up more than 6 inches and width and 7 inches in height		Typical of children and reflects immaturity in adolescents and adults. This expansiveness also reflects neurological impairment. When the neurologic status is normal, the expansiveness is scored as narcissism, immaturity, and anti-social functioning.

(*Continued*)

#	Feature	Indicated	Interpretation
14	There should always be a dividing line between the roof (or attic area) and the living area of the house in individuals. Score if there is failure to include this dividing line in individuals ages 6 and older.		Reality/fantasy disturbance (e.g., schizophrenia) and usually reflects ideational turmoil and inadequate separation between fantasy (attic area) and reality (living area).
15	Individuals of all ages may include tile lines in the roof area		When the lines are horizontal, the subject may be experiencing pressures from ego-syntonic ideation. Conversely, when the lines are drawn vertically in the roof area, the subject is likely experiencing ego-dystonic, unacceptable ideation. Meticulous roof tiling reflects excessive obsessive-compulsive tendencies.
16	Roof overhangs that protrude past wall lines		Reflects paranoid ideation
17	Roof/ attic areas are penetrated by other features (e.g., tree branches, sunrays, clouds)		Is rare and suggests disruptions that often reflect traumatic experiences.
18	Absence of a front door		Is rare and would reflect extreme isolation and mistrust. Treatment should be limited to pharmacological and crisis-intervention modalities as the relationship aspects of psychotherapy are too threatening.
19	Doors without doorknobs		Reflect resistance to self-exploration, limited insight and the perception that therapy is threatening. Short-term and brief symptom-relief treatment modalities are within the capabilities of the subject.

(Continued)

#	Feature	Indicated	Interpretation
20	Doorknob size is disproportionate to size of door		Reflects accessibility to self-exploration in treatment. The larger the size of the doorknob, the greater the accessibility to treatment.
21	Steps leading up to the door, pathway leading up to but not actually touching the baseline and patio stones in front of the doorway		Other indication of inaccessibility to a relationship and treatment.
22	A second door		Indicates ambivalence and anxiety regarding relationships and treatment. Brief, symptom-focused treatment is realistic for these individuals.
23	Doors with rounded top portions		Suggests the possibility of ideational pressure resulting from libidinal pressures.
	On rare occasions, individuals have drawn other objects inside the door outline (e.g., tree limb, bush, etc.)		Suggests sexual trauma experiences.
24	Individuals 6 years and older who drawn transparent houses		Indicative of severe ideational turmoil. The question of primary process ideational turmoil (e.g., psychosis) should be considered.
25	Breaks occur in the line(s) forming the wall(s)		Consider intermittent or episodic breaks in reality testing.
26	Windows are the opportunities to observe or be observed by others. Windows drawn within ½ inch of the roof line		Suggest fear of anyone seeing inside, which ties in with severe pathology (e.g., paranoid and schizoaffective disorders).

(Continued)

#	Feature	Indicated	Interpretation
	There is no roof line, and the windows extend up into the attic area		Suggests the severity of the pathology is more definite.
27	Picture windows and windows placed within ½ inch of ground level		Suggests exhibitionistic tendencies.
28	Vertical lines on the windows		Reflective of extreme caution and mistrust.
29	Crisscrossed or cross-hatched lines in the window		Suggests poor impulse control. If the cross-hatching lines extend past the window outline, the lack of self-criticalness, lack of guilt, and corresponding impulsivity are likely.
30	Window cross-hatching that resembles a crucifix (i.e., the horizontal line crosses intersect the vertical line above its midpoint)		Suggest severe psychopathology, particularly when other indications of major mental illness exist. "Crucifix" windows are often drawn by individuals with paranoia and paranoid schizophrenia. The less appropriate the crucifix symbol is to the drawing (e.g., as eye pupils) the greater the likelihood of the presence of severe pathology. The degree of religiosity of the subject does not affect the scoring.
31	Children often draw furniture inside the house		Indicates their high level of preoccupation or concern for that room's significance.
	A dining room table with no chairs		Suggests accentuated nurture deprivation.
	Furniture for adults is rare		Suggests more intense difficulties with regard to the dynamics raised by the furniture drawn.

(*Continued*)

#	Feature	Indicated	Interpretation
32	Additional features	–	–
	a Fences of all types are significant		Suggests guardedness, mistrust, paranoia, and poor social skills.
	Spiked Fence		Suggests aggressivity.
	b Mailbox		Raises questions about identity (i.e., who lives here?).
	c Drainpipe along the wall of the house		Suggests immaturity, passive-aggressiveness and, particularly when water is drawn coming out of the drainpipe, enuresis.
	d Clouds or Birds		Often reflect depressive overtones
	e The sun		Often suggests an attachment to father/male figures
	f Kites or Balloons in the Sky		Reflect concealed dysphoria, external pressures, and insecurity.
	g Flowers or Shrubs around the house	–	–
	Females		Emphasize the need to be seen as feminine. Often these individuals resort to role playing and manipulation in their relationships, particularly when the other person is a much older male.
	Males		Often struggling with their masculinity in conflicted and anxiety producing ways.

Tree Drawing Test (#33–47): The tree drawing test measures ideational and libidinal pressures throughout one's lifespan.

#	Feature	Indicated	Interpretation
33	Trees placed <1/2 inch of the bottom edge of the paper		Occurs most often with children and suggests appropriate security needs. The older the individual, the greater the clinical significance of a tree placed near the bottom edge, and the more insecure and dependent on external support the individual is.
34	The leaf structure extends beyond the limits of the page		Indicates poor judgment, ideational turmoil, impaired planning, and lack of forethought, a lack of self-criticalness and a strong likelihood of acting out in socially unacceptable ways.
35	Heavy or dark line shading		Suggests depression. The heavier or darker line shading reflects the degree of depression.
36	Shading made with the pencil held horizontally, like an artist would		Suggest narcissistic and manipulative tendencies, and not depression.
37	Trees vary by geographic location of testing.	–	–
	a A "spiked" tree includes pointed or dagger like branches, roots or leaf structures.		Suggests extreme anger and violence proneness. If the dagger-like portion goes off of the top or sides of the page, consider aggressive acting out.
	b If the leaves are more like thorn like than leaf like		Suggests the strong presence of premorbid anger, and that the anger is both intense and threatening to erupt.
	c Christmas trees, regardless of season		Reflect both anger and depression.

(*Continued*)

#	Feature	Indicated	Interpretation
	d "Shattered" or grossly disfigured trees (rare)		Suggest trauma and serious disturbance.
	e "Lollipop" trees (i.e., a thin, stick-like trunk with a bare round circle at the top)		Suggest dependence, neediness, and accentuated need to be taken care of. Consider chemical dependency, immaturity, and substance abuse.
38	Any distortions on the trunk (e.g., squirrel holes, branches, knot holes, vertical lines, trunk slashes or breaks in the exterior trunk lines)		Suggest trauma. The length of the trunk is viewed as representing the lifespan of the individual. For example, if a trunk is six inches long, the age of the subject in years is divided by six to suggest the age at time of trauma.
39	Roots		Usually reflect insufficient, inadequate, and traumatic nurturance in infancy.
40	Any broken branch structure that protrudes from the leaf area		Indicates the presence of ongoing primary process ideation. Leaf structures provide a measure of the individual's cognitive organization and mental processes.
41	Scribbled and disorganized leaf structures		Reflect ideational or cognitive turmoil.
42	Arrow-like projection leaves		Reflect acting out anger.
43	Branches that appear on trunks below the leaf structures		Often represent traumatic losses at approximately the ages indicated by the location of the branch on the trunk. Common losses could be loss of parent, grandparent, sibling via psychosocial factors like death, divorce, injury, illness, incarceration, or abandonment.

(*Continued*)

#	Feature	Indicated	Interpretation
44	Grass around the tree		Suggests intense libidinal interests and pressures. In these individuals, affective and libidinal pressures are intensified.
45	Addition of "nice" things on or under the leaf structure (e.g., bird's nest, swing, tire-swing, Christmas ornaments or presents)		Indicates excessive denial and repression of anger or rage.
46	Apples or other fruit drawn on the tree		Suggests nurture deprivation, depressed ideation, and unconscious dissatisfaction with self.
	Fruit has fallen on the ground		Indicates the belief that nurturance is not forthcoming.
47	The tree is barren		Expresses the ultimate in depression and self-denigration.
	Barren trees combined with a darkly shaded trunk area		Suggests self-harm potential is high and hospitalization may be necessary.

Free Drawing Test (#48–72): The free drawing test should follow the HTP Drawing Test as a means of applying a projective measure with no structure of meaning (similar to card #16 of the TAT). The more unusual the free drawing, the more pertinent the information obtained.

Instructions are simply, "Draw anything at all, except a house, a tree, or a person." Ideally, testing rooms should be free of stimuli that, seen in the office, may be reproduced in the free drawing (or Rorschach, or card 16 of TAT). If the individual does use the environment to avoid self-disclosure, the attempt is permitted and scored as resistance to self-disclosure, guardedness, and rebelliousness. What is chosen to copy and what was not chosen are also important. The dynamics involved in the chosen item are scorable (e.g., pencil sharpener scored as angry, evasive, and possibly abused).

#	Feature	Indicated	Interpretation
48	A knife		Suggests verbal, physical, and sexual aggression, particularly if there are blood drops dripping from the knife. This would reflect an individual, usually a sadistic psychopath, expressing uncritical, sadistic, and threateningly aggressive ideation. They do not care what the examiner or society thinks of them or their antisocial behavior.
49	Overelaborate drawing with or without humorous characteristics (i.e., a barnyard scene with horse, wagon, barn, rake)		Bi-polar or manic individuals. When asked what he was drawing this individual giddily told a story of a farmer who had gone to town and gotten drunk, come home, and stepped on the hoe-explaining, he didn't know his ass (donkey) from the hoe on the ground.
50	Cars, trucks, vans, or racing cars drawn by a male		Suggest movement and acting out, behavior disorder tendencies.
50a	Drawn by a female		Suggests gender confusion or disturbance.

(Continued)

#	Feature	Indicated	Interpretation
50b	Drawn by Individuals > age 40		Often aggressive and immature.
50c	Vehicles with a flat tire		Suggest accident proneness.
50d	Accentuated (in size and/ or attention to detail) rear taillights, rear-end views or extra detailing of rear portion		Reflects anal erotic pressures.
51	Boats, regardless of geographic location of assessment		Usually represent dependency features and a wish to escape from and avoid responsibilities.
51a	The absence of water to support the boat or drawing the boat suspended above the water line		Suggests a lack or nurture and ongoing pursuit of nurture, particularly in terms of mother/female figures. Consider chemical dependency.
51b	A sailboat with a mast extending off the top of the page		Suggests castration anxiety.
51c	The omission of someone steering the boat (any boat)		Suggests poor impulse control, a lack of self-criticalness, and limited insight into his or her behavior.
52	**Any** vehicle extending off of the page		Suggests poor judgment, poor planning, and acting out aggression.
53	Football fields, with ten-yard markers		Suggest obsessive-compulsive ruminations, repetitive ideation, passive-aggressive tendencies, paranoia, and dissatisfaction with conscious ideations.
53a	Drawn by a female		Suggests gender confusion.

(*Continued*)

#	Feature	Indicated	Interpretation
54	Baseball fields		Suggest a regressive fantasy, a dream, or wish to return to a responsibility-free era in childhood. The narcissistic and grandiose aspects also suggest a lack of self-confidence and a manipulative method of obtaining success.
55	Furry animals (i.e., animals that have fur, regardless of whether the fur is drawn)		Suggest strong unmet affective needs. The individual desires to be held, caressed (in a pre-pubescent, non-penetration manner), protected from harm and responsibility and nurtured are paramount
56	Threatening animals (e.g., animals that are aggressive or frightening to most people, including fictional animals in a threatening pose)		Reflect severe aggressive, dangerous ideation and actions. E.g., large, aggressive dogs, a Cobra's head, a wolf, etc., all suggest dangerousness.
57	Jewelry of all types		Reflects self-dissatisfaction and a need to obtain external reassurances of being valued. Consider depression, histrionic personality, borderline personality, and anti-social personality.
58	Cartoon figures, regardless of age of the subject		Suggest guardedness, immaturity, and acute awareness of and mistrust of the environment.
59	Landscapes or flowers		Usually drawn by depressed individuals who are feeling lonely and unwanted. Landscapes are suggestive of mother/child relationships, then, depending on the details, suggest mother as

#	Feature	Indicated	Interpretation
			giving and nurturing or rejecting and cold.
60	Flowers		Represent intense affective needs.
60a	Flowers drawn by males are rare.		Suggest affective deprivation and gender confusion.
61	Celestial objects		Usually drawn by individuals with severe reality/fantasy deficits (i.e., poor reality testing).
61a	Stars in the sky or an astrological chart		Consider psychoses and schizoaffective disorders.
61b	The moon		Reflects a symbol of femininity in terms of the menstrual cycle, thus a moon drawing suggests ongoing conflicts with mother, particularly if the moon is half or less.
61c	The sun		Suggests a strong and unresolved attachment to father, particularly when the sun is large or has rays extending outward.
62	Religious symbols		Typically drawn by psychotic individuals with illogical preoccupations with guilt, right, and wrong. Religious figures rarely draw religious symbols. The healthier the individual, the less they need to rely on external religiosity.
63	Abstract drawings like abstract art (i.e., content is vague or unrecognizable)		Usually reflects manipulation, guardedness, and resistance, particularly if drawn quickly and non-critically.

(Continued)

#	Feature	Indicated	Interpretation
63a	Intricate, compulsively detailed abstraction		Suggests severe ideational disturbance.
64	Bed(s)		Reflect sensual concerns and tendencies towards somatization and manipulation through somatic complaints.
65	Chair(s)		Suggest passivity, dependency, and passive-aggressive tendencies.
65a	An electric chair		Indicative of intense environmental stress regarding possible consequences of the individual's behavior.
65b	A throne		Suggests feelings of inferiority manifested by stereotypic, pseudo-masculine compensatory behavior.
66	Box(es)		Rare and reflect paranoid and paranoid schizophrenic disturbances. The box symbolizes a place to hide something, usually from yourself.
67	Monetary symbols (e.g., a sheath of bills wrapped with a band around the stack, paper money, coins, dollar and cent symbols)		Often reflect sociopathy and an excessive concern with money without working for it. The narcissistic sociopath's "give me this, I deserve it" is probable. Monetary symbols are suggestive of low motivation for treatment, poor insight and depression (i.e., The hopelessness in, "I must steal or win the lottery because I cannot earn it appropriately.")
68	A pot of gold at the end of the rainbow		Another monetary response. It suggests depression, with

(Continued)

#	Feature	Indicated	Interpretation
			the fantasy of a magical solution to the individual's lifelong problems.
69	Dragon(s)		Represent excessive fantasy often involving aggression and anger. Substance abuse is often associated with dragon drawings.
69a	Flame-like features		Suggest covert guilt for the individual's real or fantasized sexual behavior, for which he or she will "burn in hell."
70	Pencil(s)		Usually reflect guardedness and resistance.
70a	Pointed upward		Suggests sexual aggressivity.
70b	Pointed downward		Suggests impotence.
71	Vases with or without flowers		Suggest self-dissatisfaction, narcissism, and nurture depletion (empty-vessel syndrome).

Kinetic Family Drawing (#72–78) involves the manifest and latent content of the individual's conscious and unconscious interpersonal relations, particularly with family of origin members. The subject is asked to draw his or her family engaged in some form of activity.

#	Feature	Indicated	Interpretation
72	Order in which family members are drawn		Signifies the order of psychological importance the family member has to the individual.
73	The placement of the figures on the paper and proximity to the individual's figure.		Proximity to the individual's figure is scored as attachment (if within ½ inch) or rejection (if >1.5 inches away).
	Figures facing away from each other		Suggest rejection.
74	Parental figures drawn smaller than children		Suggest a lack of parental maturity, parental inconsistency, and a lack of adequate nurture and limit-setting by parents. Parental figures should be larger than sibling or self-presentation.
	Adults who draw self smaller than own children		Suggests rejection of adult, parental role.
75	Omission of any particular family member		Critical. Suggests serious ideational disturbance involving the missing member, including the individual.
	Adults who draw family of origin instead of spouse and children		Suggests rejection of marriage and parenting responsibilities. They are exhibiting regressive behavior with a wish to be taken care of by their own parents.
76	Family group activities		Suggest fantasized or artificial closeness.

(*Continued*)

#	Feature	Indicated	Interpretation
77	Heavy shading		Suggests depression and conscious self and other dissatisfaction.
78	Implements Included	–	–
	a Fishing poles		Phallic symbols. Poles drawn extending off of the edge of the paper suggest sexual acting out by the family member holding the pole.
	b Cooking implements		Depict nurturance from the person using them.
	c Absence of chairs around a dining table		Suggests frustrated dependency needs.
	d Swimming activities		Reflect dependency features.
	e Mirror(s) or telephone(s)		Suggest narcissism and rejection by the figure using the phone or mirror.

Draw-A-Person (#79–96) human figures reflect the individual's self-image, body-image, and interpersonal relations. Drawings by children under age eight are scorable, but less scorable than older children or adults. The individual is instructed to draw a full length person. Requests for guidance/clarification (e.g., which sex?) is scored as anxiety and dependence. If the individual draws a "stick" figure, allow it and score it as evasiveness. Then apologize and ask the person to draw another full-length person, but not a stick figure. After one figure is accomplished, take the paper away and give another sheet, then ask for a full-length person of the opposite sex.

#	Feature	Indicated	Interpretation
79	Individual draws opposite gender first		Suggests gender confusion
80	Comparison of the two figures' sizes		Much larger figures suggest the gender of the lager figure is more threatening, aggressive than the smaller figure. The significance includes the gender of the individual in terms of identification with the aggressor or the victim.
81	Accentuated (in size and/or attention to detail) ear(s)		Suggests interpersonal sensitivity, mistrust, and possible paranoia.
82	Detailed hair		Suggests excessive sexual ideation.
83	Eyes without pupils		Suggest lack of insight and possible primal scene trauma.
84	Eyes with pupils facing down		Suggests castration or penetration anxiety.
85	Lollipop heads		Suggest role-playing tendencies.
86	No necks or thick necks (proportional to head, > 1/3 of the width of the head)		Suggests stubbornness, lack of planning, or forethought.

(Continued)

#	Feature	Indicated	Interpretation
87	Heads/ necks that are not connected to the shoulders		Suggest poor reality testing and severe pathology.
88	Nude of semi-nude (no top or no bottom clothing) figures		Suggest severe pathology (e.g., schizophrenia), exhibitionism, and narcissism.
89	Transparencies (seeing the body through clothing)		Suggests schizophrenia in adolescents and adults.
90	Fingers	–	–
	a Four-fingered hand drawn by a male		Suggests castration anxiety.
	b Pointed or talon fingers		Suggests aggressivity.
	c Fists		Suggests aggressivity and passive-aggressive tendencies.
91	Wrist lines		Suggest depression and possible self-harm.
92	Dark lines		Suggest anger and hostility (verbal or physical).
93	Clothing Features	–	–
	a Buttons drawn by adolescents and adults (ages 13+)		Suggest accentuated dependency features.
	b A tie drawn by male adults on the male figure		Suggests insecurity, inadequacy, and sexual concerns.
	c Pockets on the shirt/ blouse or pants drawn by adolescents or adults (ages 13+)		Suggests exaggerated dependency features.
	d High heels or overly detailed shoes		Suggest obsessive-compulsive defenses and passive-aggressive tendencies.

(Continued)

#	Feature	Indicated	Interpretation
	e Purses or briefcases		Suggest feelings of inadequacy and covert aggressivity.
94	Open mouths or mouths without teeth		Suggest exaggerated oral dependency needs, cutting sarcasm, and addiction-proneness.
95	Facial scars		Suggest deviant dependency features and antisocial tendencies.
96	Small noses (proportional to face, ≤ 1/6 of face)		Suggest feelings of inadequacy, powerlessness, and self-dissatisfaction.

Appendix B
House Drawing Inquiry Phase Sample Questions

The following are sample questions the examiner may ask, in addition to any other questions indicated by the participant's behavior during administration and/or notable features of the drawing. The following list is neither mandatory nor exhaustive. Clinicians are encouraged to use clinical judgment in determining the appropriateness of questions asked during the optional inquiry phase.

1   How many stories does this house have?
2   Have you seen that house before?
3   What does that house remind you of?
4   Would you like to live in that house?
5   Which room would you take for your own?
6   Who would you like to live in that house with you?
7   Is that house close or far away?
8   What does that house need most?

Appendix C
Tree Drawing Inquiry Phase Sample Questions

The following are sample questions the examiner may ask, in addition to any other questions indicated by the participant's behavior during administration and/or notable features of the drawing. The following list is neither mandatory nor exhaustive. Clinicians are encouraged to use clinical judgment in determining the appropriateness of questions asked during the optional inquiry phase.

1 What kind of tree is that?
2 Were is that tree?
3 How old is that tree?
4 Is the tree alive? What makes it look alive (or not alive)?
5 Is the tree by itself or in a group of trees?
6 Who does that tree remind you of?
7 What does that tree need most?
8 What is the weather like in this picture?

Appendix D
Person Drawing Inquiry Phase Sample Questions

For the two Human Figure drawings, begin the inquiry phase as follows: "Please make up an interesting story about this person, and should not be anyone you know." The following questions can be used to gather more projections from the drawing, but this list is not exhaustive; the clinician is encouraged to use clinical judgment in developing hypotheses and follow-up questions based on the participant's unique intra-individual factors and any notable features of the drawing.

1 How old is the person?
2 What is she or he doing now?
3 What is she or he thinking?
4 What is she or he feeling?
5 What was she or he doing before this?
6 What will she or he do next?
7 If the person has three wishes, what will they be:

   a.
   b.
   c.

Appendix E
Kinetic Family Drawing Inquiry Phase Sample Questions

The following are sample questions the examiner may ask, in addition to any other questions indicated by the participant's behavior during administration and/or notable features of the drawing. The following list is neither mandatory nor exhaustive. Clinicians are encouraged to use clinical judgment in determining the appropriateness of questions asked during the optional inquiry phase.

1   Tell me about this picture?
2   What is [each figure] doing?
3   What is [each figure] feeling?
4   What might happen next?

Appendix F
Quantitative Interpretation of The RGBGT

The following 207 interpretations are the psychological and neuro-psychological interpretations that correspond to the scorable errors made by the examinee. These interpretations are positive diagnostic considerations and not DSM-IVR diagnoses. These objective findings must be considered within the wider context of the overall psychological, neuropsychological and psychoeducational test results, interview data, and other ancillary data (i.e., academic and medical records). The 11 Experimental Items (Item number preceded by the letter E) are still in various stages of research.

Interpretation of these distortions, though valid in the authors' opinions, should be made more cautiously until that research has been completed and published.

All interpretations are grouped into general diagnostic and behavioral considerations using the individual interpretations arising from each design, as well as overall reproduction distortions. Within each of these ten areas, preliminary conclusions can be reached based upon the preponderance of the evidence for that clinical area. These conclusions can then be combined, taking into account the frequency of the specific findings, clinical issues, and background. This is a scoring process that is improved by usage, clinical experience, and knowledge. However, students and neophyte clinicians can obtain highly complex and relevant data from the scoring system.

Specific Design Interpretations:

Overall Design Distortions and Interpretations

Item No.	*Distortion and Interpretation*
1.	All nine designs are drawn in the upper half of one page: ***Adults & Adolescents (16–80 years of age):*** *Sociopathy. Artificial impulse control. Acting out tendencies. Defective ego. Lack of self criticism. Lack of empathy.* ***Children (8–15 years of age):*** *Acting out tendencies. Conduct disorder. Lack of self-criticism. Lack of empathy.*
2.	At a minimum, Cards A, 1 and 2 are drawn using the right hand margin rather than the left margin of the page: ***Adults & Adolescents (16–80 years of age):*** *Sociopathy. Extreme negativism. Rebelliousness. Anti-social. Violence prone.* ***Children (8–15 years of age):*** *Extreme negativism. Rebelliousness. Anti-social. Violence prone. Conduct disorder.*
3.	The use of a second page begins with Design 2: ***All Ages:*** *Possible instructional problem. Clarify instructions. Consider neurologic deficits.*
4.	The use of a second page begins with Design 3: ***All Ages:*** *Possible instructional problem. Clarify instructions. Consider personality factors.*
5.	The use of a second page begins with Design 4: ***Adults & Adolescents (16–80 years of age):*** *Anxiety related to interpersonal functioning in general, and intimate functioning in particular. Inadequate separation from the parental figures. Immaturity.* ***Children (8–15 years of age):*** Anxiety related to interpersonal functioning in general. Inadequate separation from the parental figures.
6.	The use of a second page begins with Design 5: ***Adults & Adolescents (16–80 years of age):*** *Exaggerated dependency. Immaturity. Anxiety. Avoidance of intimacy.* ***Children (8–15 years of age):*** *Exaggerated dependency. Anxiety. Avoidance of intimacy.*
7.	There is the use of more than two (3 or more) pages to draw the designs: ***Adults & Adolescents (16–80 years of age):*** *Possible instructional problem. Clarify instructions. Possible psychosis. Grandiosity. Expansiveness. Narcissism. Inadequate impulse control.* ***Children (8–15 years of age):*** *Possible instructional problem. Clarify instructions. Possible psychosis. Grandiosity. Expansiveness.*

(Continued)

Item No.	Distortion and Interpretation

8. The designs are numbered and/or compartmentalized with the use of lines as boundaries:
All Ages:
Attempts to maintain the appearance of better impulse control than actually exists. Role playing.

9. Card A comes within 1/4 inch or goes off any edge of the paper:
Adults & Adolescents (16–80 years of age):
Non-compliance with authority figures (i.e., parents). Acting out tendencies. Poor impulse control. Exaggerated dependency needs. Gross immaturity.
Children (8–15 years of age):
Non-compliance with authority figures (i.e., parents). Acting out tendencies. Poor impulse control.

10. Card 1 comes within 1/4 inch or goes off any edge of the paper:
Adults & Adolescents (16–80 years of age):
Inadequate impulse control. Acting out tendencies. Requires external limit setting on behavior. Possible psychopathy or sociopathy. Violence-prone.
Children (8–15 years of age):
Inadequate impulse control. Acting out tendencies. Violence-prone.

11. Card 2 comes within 1/4 inch or goes off any edge of the paper:
Adults & Adolescents (16–80 years of age):
Affect-driven. Labile. Emotionally and behaviorally temperamental. Volatile. Possible bipolar disorder or borderline personality disorder.
Children (8–15 years of age):
Affect-driven. Labile. Emotionally and behaviorally temperamental. Volatile.

12. Card 3 comes within 1/4 inch or goes off any edge of the paper:
Adults & Adolescents (16–80 years of age):
Violence prone. Physically and sexually aggressive. Immature. Consider sexual psychopathy, pedophilia, sociopathy or psychopathy.
Children (8–15 years of age):
Violence prone. Physically and sexually aggressive.

13 Card 4 comes within 1/4 inch or goes off any edge of the paper:
All Ages:
Socially isolated. Poor peer relationships. Intense anger with acting out potential. Argumentative. Infantile. Rebellious. Rule-breaking.

14 Card 5 comes within 1/4 inch or goes off any edge of the paper:
Adults & Adolescents (16–80 years of age):
Impulsivity. Gross immaturity. Promiscuity. Acting out tendencies. Consider schizophrenia, psychopathy, sociopathy, or borderline personality disorder.
Children (8–15 years of age):
Impulsivity. Promiscuity. Acting out tendencies. Consider schizophrenia or conduct disorder.

(Continued)

Item No.	Distortion and Interpretation

15. Card 5: The straight row of dots comes within 1/4 inch or goes off the top of the page:
Adults & Adolescents (16–80 years of age):
Seeks environmental limits on acting out behavior (i.e., promiscuity).
Children (8–15 years of age):
Seeks environmental limits on acting out behavior.

16. Card 6: The horizontal line comes within 1/4.inch or goes off either side of the paper:
Adults & Adolescents (16–80 years of age):
Interacts with others in terms of overwhelming and insatiable affective needs. Demanding of nurture, attention and affect from others. Consider narcissistic, borderline, histrionic, dependent and anti-social personality disorders.
Children (8–15 years of age):
Interacts with others in terms of overwhelming and insatiable affective needs. Demanding of nurture, attention and affect from others.

17. Card 6: The vertical line comes within 1/4 inch or goes off the top of the paper:
All Ages:
Acting out intense emotion (i.e., rage). Potentially dangerous (i.e., assault, homicide). May deny, suppress and displace rage (i.e., somatization).

18. Card 6: The vertical line comes within 1/4 inch or goes off the bottom of the page:
All Ages):
Severe depression. Intrapunitive and suicidal tendencies. Possibility of self-harm should be seriously considered.

19. Card 7 comes within 1/4 inch or goes off any edge of the paper:
Adults & Adolescents (16–80 years of age):
Acting out. Dangerous. Possible organic impairment. Consider psychopathy or sociopathy.
Children (8–15 years of age):
Acting out. Dangerous. Consider conduct disorder.

20. Card 8 comes within 1/4 inch or goes off any edge of the paper:
Adults & Adolescents (16–80 years of age):
Behavioral and ideational turmoil. Sexual aggressivity. Sexual trauma. Consider psychosis, psychopathy, sociopathy and imminent dangerousness.
Children (8–15 years of age):
Behavioral and ideational turmoil. Aggressivity. Trauma. Consider psychosis and imminent dangerousness.

21. There is a collision or near collision between Designs A & 1 (i.e., Designs overlap or come within 1/4 inch of each other):
Adults & Adolescents (16–80 years of age):
Acting out tendencies toward parental and authority figures. Rebelliousness. Intense, chronic negativism. Immaturity. Possible sociopathy; psychopathy and conduct disorders in adolescence.

(Continued)

Item No.	Distortion and Interpretation
	Children (8–15 years of age): *Acting out tendencies toward parental and authority figures. Rebelliousness. Intense, chronic negativism. Possible conduct disorders in adolescence.*
22.	There is a collision or near collision between Designs A & 2 (i.e., Designs overlap or come within 1/4 inch of each other): **Adults & Adolescents (16–80 years of age):** *Severe depression and self-dissatisfaction secondary to unresolved conflicts with parental/authority figures. Unmet dependency needs. Possible bereavement.* **Children (8–15 years of age):** *Severe depression and self-dissatisfaction secondary to ongoing conflicts with parental/authority figures. Possible bereavement.*
23.	There is a collision or near collision between Designs A & 3 (i.e., Designs overlap or come within 1/4 inch of each other): **All Ages:** *Trauma in relation to parental/authority figures. Intense hostility from and/or toward parental/authority figures.*
24.	There is a collision or near collision between Designs A & 4 (i.e., Design's overlap or come within 1/4 inch of each other): **Adults & Adolescents (16–80 years of age):** *Excessive dependency on parental figures. Lack of sufficient separation and individuation. Immaturity. Consider borderline and dependent personality disorders.* **Children (8–15 years of age):** *Excessive dependency on parental figures. Lack of sufficient age-appropriate separation and individuation.*
25.	There is a collision or near collision between Designs A & 5 (i.e., Designs overlap or come within 1/4 inch of each other): **Adults & Adolescents (16–80 years of age):** *Excessive dependency. Trauma. Consider psychosis, psychopathy, sociopathy, or schizophrenia.* **Children (8–15 years of age):** *Excessive dependency. Trauma. Consider psychosis or other severe disorder.*
26	There is a collision or near collision between Designs A & 6 (i.e., Designs overlap or come within 1/4 inch of each other): **All Ages:** *Severe depression to psychotic levels. Unresolved dependency issues with parental/authority figures. Overt conflicts with authority figures. Intense hostility. Dangerousness to self or others.*
27.	There is a collision or near collision between Designs A & 7 (i.e., Designs overlap or come within 1/4 inch of each other): **All Ages:** *Ideational turmoil in relation to parental/authority figures. Intense hostility from and/or toward parental/authority figures. Possible neurologic impairment.*

(Continued)

Item No.	Distortion and Interpretation

28. There is a collision or near collision between Designs A & 8 (i.e., Designs overlap or come within 1/4 inch of each other):
    All Ages:
    Sexual or other trauma in connection with parental/authority figures. Intense hostility from and/or toward parental/authority figures.

29. There is a collision or near collision between Designs 1 & 2 (i.e., Designs overlap or come within 1/4 inch of each other):
    Adults & Adolescents (16–80 years of age):
    Self-punitive acting out. Active suicidal ideations and tendencies. Poor impulse control. Depression at or near psychotic levels. Poor judgment.
    Children (8–15 years of age):
    Self-punitive acting out. Active suicidal ideations and tendencies. Poor impulse control. Depression at or near psychotic levels.

30. There is a collision or near collision between Designs 1 & 3 (i.e., Designs overlap or come within 1/4 inch of each other):
    Adults & Adolescents (16–80 years of age):
    Consider psychopathy, sociopathy, intense hostility, inadequate impulse control mechanisms, sexual and aggressive acting out. Possible sexual predator tendencies.
    Children (8–15 years of age):
    Consider conduct disorder, intense hostility, inadequate impulse control mechanisms, sexual and aggressive acting out.

31. There is a collision or near collision between Designs 1 & 4 (i.e., Designs overlap or come within 1/4 inch of each other):
    Adults & Adolescents (16–80 years of age):
    Immaturity. Exaggerated dependency on parental/authority figures. Intense hostility. Severe peer relationship disturbances.
    Children (8–15 years of age):
    Exaggerated dependency on parental/authority figures. Intense hostility. Severe peer relationship disturbances.

32. There is a collision or near collision between Designs 1 & 5 (i.e., Designs overlap or come within 1/4 inch of each other):
    Adults & Adolescents (16–80 years of age):
    Consider psychopathy, socfopathy, psychosis, aggressivity and addiction-proneness.
    Children (8–15 years of age):
    Consider psychosis, aggressivity and addiction-proneness.

33. There is a collision or near collision between Designs 1 & 6 (i.e., Designs overlap or come within 1/4 inch of each other):
    All Ages:
    Suicidal tendencies. Borderline to psychotic functioning. Unpredictable acting out tendencies.

34. There is a collision or near collision between Designs 1 & 7 (i.e., Designs overlap or come within. 1/4 inch of each other):
    All Ages:
    Neurological deficits. Overwhelming sexual ideation and acting out potential. Very poor impulse control. Consider psychosis, schizophrenia, neurologic impairment.

(Continued)

Item No.	Distortion and Interpretation
35.	There is a collision or near collision between Designs 1 & 8 (i.e., Designs overlap or come within 1/4 inch of each other): ***Adults & Adolescents (16–80 years of age):*** *Possiqle sexual trauma. Combination of sexual and aggressive behavioral functioning. Gross immaturity. Severe relationship difficulties.* ***Children (8–15 years of age):*** *Possible sexual trauma. Combination of sexual and aggressive behavioral functioning. Severe relationship difficulties.*
36.	There is a collision or near collision between Designs 2 & 3 (i.e., Designs overlap or come within. 1/4 inch of each other): ***Adults & Adolescents (16–80 years of age):*** *Extremely high acting out potential. Dangerousness. Accentuated self-dissatisfaction. Possible self-harm potential. Affect driven. Impulsivity.* ***Children (8–15 years of age):*** *Extremely high acting out potential. Dangerousness. Accentuated self-dissatisfaction. Possible self-harm potential. Affect driven.*
37.	There is a collision or near collision between Designs 2 & 4 (i.e., Designs overlap or come within 1/4 inch of each other): ***Adults & Adolescents (16–80 years of age):*** *Severe depression. Overt, conscious self-dissatisfaction with high self-harm potential. Unresolved dependency. Poor self-esteem.* ***Children (8–15 years of age):*** *Severe depression. Overt, conscious self-dissatisfaction with high self-harm potential. Poor self-esteem.*
38.	There is a collision or near collision between Designs 2 & 5 (i.e., Designs overlap or come within 1/4 inch of each other): ***Adults & Adolescents (16–80 years of age):*** *Consider psychosis, psychopathy, sociopathy and borderline personality functioning. Exacerbated depressive features. Possible dissociative processes. Extreme anger.* ***Children (8–15 years of age):*** *Consider psychosis and borderline personality functioning. Exacerbated depressive features. Possible dissociative processes. Extreme anger.*
39.	There is a collision or near collision between Designs 2 & 6 (i.e., Designs overlap or come within 1/4 inch of each other): ***All Ages:*** *Severe depression with suicidal tendencies. Accentuated hostility. Affect driven.*
40.	There is a collision or near collision between Designs 2 & 7 (i.e., Designs overlap or come within, 1/4 inch of each other): ***All Ages:*** *Neurologic deficits. Affect driven. Preoccupation with disturbed ideation. Psychotic depression. Gross ideational and behavioral turmoil.*

(Continued)

Item No.	Distortion and Interpretation

41. There is a collision or near collision between Designs 2 & 8 (i.e., Designs overlap or come within 1/4 inch of each other):
    Adults & Adolescents (16–80 years of age):
    Neurologic deficits. Self-dissatisfaction. Immaturity. Dysphoria. Gross dysfunction with intimacy.
    Children (8–15 years of age):
    Neurologic deficits. Self-dissatisfaction. Dysphoria.

42. There is a collision or near collision between Designs 3 & 4 (i.e., Designs overlap or come within 1/4 inch of each other):
    Adults & Adolescents (16–80 years of age):
    Accentuated hostility. Immaturity. Peer relationship deficits. Excessive dependency. Difficulties with intimacy.
    Children (8–15 years of age):
    Accentuated hostility. Peer relationship deficits. Excessive dependency.

43. There is a collision or near collision between Designs 3 & 5 (i.e., Designs overlap or come within 1/4 inch of each other):
    Adults & Adolescents (16–80 years of age):
    Acting out tendencies. Aggressivity. Dysfunction with intimacy. Exacerbated dependency issues. Poor insight and judgment.
    Children (8–15 years of age):
    Acting out tendencies. Aggressivity. Exacerbated dependency issues. Poor judgment.

44. There is a collision or near collision between Designs 3 & 6 (i.e., Designs overlap or come within 1/4 inch of each other):
    Adults & Adolescents (16–80 years of age):
    Intense hostility. Affect driven. Severe depression. Dysfunction with intimacy. Possible suicidal/homicidal tendencies. Dangerous to self and others.
    Children (8–15 years of age):
    Intense hostility. Affect driven. Severe depression. Possible suicidal/ homicidal tendencies. Dangerous to self and others.

45. There is a collision or near collision between Designs 3 & 7 (i.e., Designs overlap or come within 1/4 inch of each other):
    Adults & Adolescents (16–80 years of age):
    Neurologic deficits. Consider psychosis. Intense hostility. Dysfunction with intimacy. Acting out tendencies. Dangerous to self and others.
    Children (8–15 years of age):
    Neurologic deficits. Consider psychosis. Intense hostility. Acting out tendencies. Dangerous to self and others.

46. There is a collision or near collision between Designs 3 & 8 (i.e., Designs overlap or come within 1/4 inch of each other):
    Adults & Adolescents (16–80 years of age):
    Neurologic deficits. Immaturity. Low frustration tolerance. Exaggerated hostility. Dysfunction with intimacy. Intense generalized anxiety.

(Continued)

Item No.	Distortion and Interpretation

<table>
<tr><td></td><td><u>*Childrett (8–15 years of age):*</u>
Neurologic deficits, Immaturity. Low frustration tolerance.
Exaggerated hostility. Intense generalized anxiety.</td></tr>
<tr><td>47.</td><td>There is a collision or near collision between Designs 4 & 5 (i.e., Designs overlap or come within 1/4 inch of each other):
<u>***Adults & Adolescents (16–80 years of age):***</u>
Severe peer relationship disturbances. Gross immaturity. Acting out tendencies. Consider psychopathy, sociopathy, schizophrenia. Possibility of trauma.
<u>***Children (8–15 years of age):***</u>
Severe peer relationship disturbances. Gross immaturity. Acting out tendencies. Possibility of trauma.</td></tr>
<tr><td>48.</td><td>There is a collision or near collision between Designs 4 & 6 (i.e., Designs overlap or come within 1/4 inch of each other):
<u>***All Ages:***</u>
Neurologic deficits. Isolation. Peer relationship disturbances. Depression. Excessive dependency. Anger prone. Affective turmoil.</td></tr>
<tr><td>49.</td><td>There is a collision or near collision behveen Designs 4 & 7 (i.e., Designs overlap or come within 1/4 inch of each other):
<u>***Adults & Adolescents (16–80 years of age):***</u>
Neurological impairment. Intense generalized anxiety. Peer relationship disturbances. Excessive dependency. Dangerous. Dysfunction with intimacy. Consider psychosis.
<u>***Children (8–15 years of age):***</u>
Neurological impairment. Intense generalized anxiety. Peer relationship disturbances. Excessive dependency. Dangerous. Consider psychosis.</td></tr>
<tr><td>50.</td><td>There is a collision or near collision between Designs 4 & 8 (i.e., Designs overlap or come within 1/4 inch of each other):
<u>***Adults & Adolescents (16–80 years of age):***</u>
Neurologic deficits. Dysfunction in intimacy. Possible trauma. Immaturity. Extreme dependency. Peer relationship disturbances.
<u>***Children (8–15 years of age):***</u>
Neurologic deficits. Possible trauma. Extreme dependency. Peer relationship disturbances.</td></tr>
<tr><td>51.</td><td>There is a collision or near collision between Designs 5 & 6 (i.e., Designs overlap or come within 1/4 inch of each other):
<u>***Adults & Adolescents (16–80 years of age):***</u>
Overwhelming affective disturbance. Depression. Aggressivity. Dangerousness. Consider psychopathy, sociopathy, bi-polar psychosis or schizophrenia.
<u>***Children (8–15 years of age):***</u>
Overwhelming affective disturbance. Depression. Aggressivity. Dangerousness. Consider conduct disorder, bi-polar psychosis or schizophrenia.</td></tr>
<tr><td>52.</td><td>There is a collision or near collision between Designs 5 & 7 (i.e., Designs overlap or come within 1/4 inch of each other):</td></tr>
</table>

(Continued)

Item No.	*Distortion and Interpretation*

> *Adults & Adolescents (16–80 years of age):*
> Neurological impairment. Affective turmoil. Exacerbated
> dependency. Possible trauma. Dysfunction with intimacy. Severe
> depression. Consider schizophrenia.
> *Children (8–15 years of age):*
> Neurological impairment. Affective turmoil. Exacerbated dependency.
> Possible trauma. Severe depression. Consider schizophrenia.

53. There is a collision or near collision between Designs 5 & 8 (i.e.,
Designs overlap or come within 1/4 inch of each other):
> *Adults & Adolescents (16–80 years of age):*
> *Possible neurological impairment. Dysfunction with intimacy.*
> *Immaturity. Consider schizophrenia.*
> *Children (8–15 years of age):*
> *Possible neurological impairment. Consider schizophrenia.*

54. There is a collision or near collision between Designs 6 & 7 (i.e.,
Designs overlap or come within 1/4 inch of each other):
> *Adults & Adolescents (16–80 years of age):*
> *Possible neurological impairment. Severe depression. Possible*
> *psychotic processes. Intense anxiety. Dysfunction with intimacy.*
> *Possible trauma.*
> *Children (8–15 years of age):*
> *Possible neurological impairment. Severe depression. Possible*
> *psychotic processes. Intense anxiety. Possible trauma.*

55. There is a collision or near collision between Designs 6 & 8 (i.e.,
Designs overlap or come within 1/4 inch of each other):
> *Adults & Adolescents (16–80 years of age):*
> *Possible neurological impairment. Severe depression. Possible*
> *psychotic processes. Intense anxiety. Immaturity. Dysfunction with*
> *intimacy. Possible trauma.*
> *Children (8–15 years of age):*
> *Possible neurological impairment. Severe depression. Possible*
> *psychotic processes. Intense anxiety. Possible trauma.*

56. There is a collision or near collision between Designs 7 & 8 (i.e.,
Designs overlap or come within 1/4 inch of each other):
> *Adults & Adolescents (16–80 years of age):*
> *Possible neurological impairment. Preoccupation with intimate*
> *ideation. Overwhelming anxiety. Immaturity. Merger of sexual and*
> *aggressive behavior. Dangerousness. Possible trauma.*
> *Children (8–15 years of age):*
> *Possible neurological impairment. Overwhelming anxiety.*
> *Dangerousness. Possible trauma.*

57. A majority of the designs (5 or more) are drawn very lightly/faintly (i.e.,
Pencil pressure is minimal):
> *Adults & Adolescents (16–80 years of age):*
> *Passivity. Intense generalized anxiety. Self-consciousness.*
> *Interpersonal avoidance; Inadequacy. Immaturity. Suppression of*
> *affect. Withdrawal. Depression.*

(Continued)

Item No.	Distortion and Interpretation

Children (8–15 years of age):
Passivity. Intense generalized anxiety. Inadequacy. Suppression of affect. Withdrawal. Depression.

58. Design A is more lightly shaded than all others:
Adults & Adolescents (16–80 years of age):
Estrangement from parental/authority figures. Repression and denial related to the importance of parental figures. Pseudo-independence. Anxiety related to unresolved dependency issues. Passivity. Immaturity.
Children (8–15 years of age):
Estrangement from parental/authority figures. Repression and denial related to the importance of parental figures. Pseudo-independence. Anxiety related to unresolved dependency issues. Passivity.

59. Design 1 is more lightly shaded than all others:
Adults & Adolescents (16–80 years of age):
Tenuous and artificial impulse control. Propensity toward acting out with passive aggressive and passive-obstructive behaviors.
Children (8–15 years of age):
Propensity toward acting out with passive-aggressive and passive-obstructive behaviors.

60. Design 2 is more lightly shaded than all others:
Adults & Adolescents (16–80 years of age):
Exaggerated dependency. Conscious dissatisfaction. Intense feelings of inadequacy and anxiety.
Children (8–15 years of age):
Conscious dissatisfaction. Intense feelings of inadequacy and anxiety.

61. Design 3 is more lightly shaded than all others:
Adults & Adolescents (16–80 years of age):
Repressed hostility. Anxiery; Self-esteem difficulties. Avoidance. of intimacy.
Children (8–15 years of age):
Repressed hostility. Anxiety; Self-esteem difficulties.

62. Design 4 is more lightly shaded than all others:
All Ages:
Disturbance of peer-relationships. Intense anxiety. Introversion. Shyness. Passivity. Prolonged and exaggerated dependency on parental/authority figures.

63. Design 5 is more lightly shaded than all others:
Adults & Adolescents (16–80 years of age):
Subtle dependency processes. Isolation. Withdrawal. Passivity. Avoidance of intimacy.
Children (8–15 years of age):
Subtle dependency processes. Isolation. Withdrawal. Passivity.

64. Design 6 is more lightly shaded than all others:
All Ages:
Suppression of affect. Passivity. Anxiety. Introversion.

(Continued)

Item No.	Distortion and Interpretation

65. Design 7 is more lightly shaded than all others:
Adults & Adolescents (16–80 years of age):
Anxiety related to intimacy. Anhedonia. Prepubescent psychosexual functioning. Immaturity.
Children (8–15 years of age):
Anxiety related to intimacy. Anhedonia. Precociousness.

66. Design 8 is more lightly shaded than all others:
Adults & Adolescents (16–80 years of age):
Isolation. Depression. Anxiety. Psychosexual immaturity. Possible sexual trauma. Anhedonia.
Children (8–15 years of age):
Isolation. Depression. Anxiety. Possible trauma. Anhedonia.

67. Design A is more darkly shaded than all others (Heavy pencil pressure):
Adults & Adolescents (16–80 years of age):
Intense anger to/from parental/authority figures. Acting out tendencies. Consider sociopathy; psychopathy; dangerousness. Inability to accept a subordinate role. Conflict with authorities.
Children (8–15 years of age):
Intense anger to/from parental/authority figures. Acting out tendencies. Consider dangerousness. Conflict with authorities.

68. Design A and Design 4 are both more darkly shaded than all others (Heavy pencil pressure):
Adults & Adolescents (16–80 years of age):
Intense anger. Difficulty maintaining a supportive role. Difficulty collaborating. Conflicts with authority figures.
Children (8–15 years of age):
Intense anger. Difficulty collaborating. Conflicts with authority figures.

69. Design 1 is more darkly shaded than all others (Heavy pencil pressure):
Adults & Adolescents (16–80 years of age):
Poor impulse control. Acting out tendencies, including aggressive acting out. Consider sociopathy, psychopathy, borderline personality functioning.
Children (8–15 years of age):
Acting out tendencies, including aggressive acting out. Consider conduct disorder and borderline personality functioning.

70. Design 2 is more darkly shaded than all others (e.g., Heavy pencil pressure):
Adults & Adolescents (16–80 years of age):
Overwhelming depression. Gross dependency features. Intense conscious self dissatisfaction. Pronounced anger.
Children (8–15 years of age):
Overwhelming depression. Intense conscious self-dissatisfaction. Pronounced anger.

71. Design 3 is more darkly shaded than all others (Heavy pencil pressure):
Adults & Adolescents (16–80 years of age):
Intense overt hostility toward father/male authority figures. Consider sociopathy, psychopathy, sexual aggressivity. Possible sexual predator.

(Continued)

Item No.	Distortion and Interpretation
	Children (8–15 years of age):
	Intense overt hostility toward father/male authority figures. Consider conduct disorder and sexual aggressivity.
72.	Design 4 is more darkly shaded than all others (Heavy pencil pressure):
	Adults & Adolescents (16–80 years of age):
	Intense anger toward parental and authority figures. Severe peer relationship disturbances. Infantile. Acting out tendencies likely. Consider sociopathy, psychopathy; borderline and narcissistic personality disorders.
	Children (8–15 years of age):
	Intense anger toward parental and authority figures. Severe peer relationship disturbances. Infantile. Acting out tendencies likely.
73.	Design 5 is more darkly shaded than all others (Heavy pencil pressure):
	Adults & Adolescents (16–80 years of age):
	Exaggerated dependency. Conflicts with intimacy. Dysfunction with intimacy. Excessive dependency, particularly toward mother/female figures. Hostility over unmet dependency needs.
	Children (8–15 years of age):
	Exaggerated dependency. Excessive dependency, particularly toward mother/female figures. Hostility over unmet dependency needs.
74.	Design 6 is more darkly shaded than all others (Heavy pencil pressure):
	All Ages:
	Affect-driven. Hostile. Depression. Anxiety. Potential dangerousness.
75.	Design 7 is more darkly shaded than all others (Heavy pencil pressure):
	Adults & Adolescents (16–80 years of age):
	Gross interpersonal turmoil. Possible sexual acting out. Possible sexual trauma. Potential dangerousness.
	Children (8–15 years of age):
	Gross interpersonal tumzoil. Possible acting out. Possible trauma. Potential dangerousness.
76.	Design 8 is more darkly shaded than all others (Heavy pencil pressure):
	Adults & Adolescents (16–80 years of age):
	Anger associated with intimacy. Severe Dysfunction with intimacy. Possible deviant sexual acting out. Possible sexual trauma. Dangerousness. Consider merger of sexual and aggressive behavior.
	Children (8–15 years of age):
	Anger. Possible deviant acting out. Possible trauma. Dangerousness.

Card A

77.	Card A: The top of the circle is drawn higher on the page than the top of the diamond:
	All Ages:
	Female/mother figure is/was the dominant, psychological parent figure.
78.	Card A: The top of the diamond is drawn higher than the top of the circle:
	All Ages:
	Male/father figure is/was the dominant, psychological parent figure.

(Continued)

Item No.	Distortion and Interpretation

79. No longer included in the scoring system.

80. Card A: The lines of the diamond penetrate the circle by any amount:
    Adults & Adolescents (16–80 years of age):
    Exposure to interparental aggression, including verbal and/or physical aggressivity. Insecurity. Generalized anxiety. Problems with intimacy. Possible aggressivity.
    Children (8–15 years of age):
    Exposure to interparental aggression, including verbal and/or physical aggressivity. Insecurity. Generalized anxiety. Possible aggressivity.

81. Card A: Either figure appears elongated or appears to be pulling away from the point of intersection (i.e., one shape is more than 1 1/2 times the length of the other):
    All Ages:
    Interparental intimacy strained and conflict-ridden (i.e., separation and/or divorce). Insecurity. Anxiety. Relationship difficulties.

82. Card A: The lines of the circle and the lines of the diamond do not touch each other at any point. The figures are completely separated:
    All Ages:
    Separated, uninvolved parental figures. High interparental conflict. Problems with relationships.

83. Card A: The lines of the circle are incomplete (i.e., There are overlapping lines, incomplete, broken lines, projecting lines, ending lines that do not meet):
    All Ages:
    Females Only: Deficient nurture by the female/mother figure. Psychasthenia. Depression. Insecurity. Self-esteem deficits and self-dissatisfaction.
    Males Only: Deficient nurture by the female/mother figure. Dependency. Interpersonal conflicts. Hostility towards females. Depression.

84. Card A: The lines of the diamond are incomplete (i.e., there are overlapping lines, incomplete, broken lines, projecting lines, ending lines that do not meet):
    All Ages:
    Females only: Deficient nurture by the male/father figure. Relationship difficulties. Excessive anger and mistrust of males. Self-esteem deficits. Self-dissatisfaction.
    Males only: Deficient nurture by the male/father figure. Feelings of inadequacy. Self dissatisfaction. Dependency. Anxiety. Self-esteem deficits.

85. Card A: The circle has a line projecting from the bottom third of the circle:
    All Ages:
    Domineering, aggressive female/mother figure. Anxiety. Self-esteem deficits. Accentuated hostility. Unresolved dependency issues. Feelings of inadequacy.

(Continued)

Item No.	*Distortion and Interpretation*

86.   Card A: There is less than a 90 degree angle at any of the four corners of the diamond (i.e., there are exaggeratedly sharpened or darkened points on the diamond):
All Ages:
Accentuated hostility from the male/father/authority figure. Hostility. Anxiety. Acting out. Depression.

87.   Card A figures are drawn below the top third of the page and all the other 8 designs are drawn below Card A:
Adults (21 and older) only:
Excessive dependency. Anxiety. Immaturity. Excessive attachment to one or both parental figures.

88.   Card A figures are drawn in the middle of the page surrounded by the other 8 designs:
Adults (21 and older) only:
Gross immaturity. Overwhelming turmoil involving unresolved dependency on one or both parental figures.

89.   Card A: The line quality of the circle fluctuates (dark to light, vice-versa):
All Ages:
Female/mother figure unreliable and inconsistent. Ambivalence. Anxiety. Insecurity. Dependency.

90.   Cad A: The line quality of the diamond fluctuates (dark to light, vice-versa):
All Ages:
Views male/father figure as unreliable and inconsistent. Ambivalence. Anxiety. Insecurity. Dependency.

91.   Card A: At least 75% of the entire circle is drawn darker than the diamond, the diamond is drawn appropriately:
All Ages:
Intensified hostility to and from the female/mother figure. Lack of nurturance from female/mother figure. Feelings of inadequacy. Difficulty with authority figures. Anger proneness.

92.   Card A: At least 75% of the entire diamond is drawn darker than the circle, the circle is drawn appropriately:
All Ages:
Intensified hostility to and from the male/father figure. Lack of nurturance from male/father figure. Feelings of inadequacy. Difficulty with authority figures. Anger proneness.

93.   Card A: Failure to draw the four-sided figure at any angle:
Adults & Adolescents (16–80 years of age):
Neurological impairment. Cerebral dysfunction. Consider retardation and dementia.
Children (8–15 years of age):
Neurological impairment. Consider fine-motor delay, retardation or cerebral deficits.

94.   Card A: There is an extreme inability to draw the diamond. The diamond drawn is unrecognizable as a diamond:

(*Continued*)

Item No.	Distortion and Interpretation

	Adults & Adolescents (16–80 years of ago): Consider retardation and severe cerebral dysfunction. *Children (8–15 years of age):* Consider fine-motor delay, retardation or cerebral deficits.
95.	Card A is drawn at least 25% smaller than Designs 3, 4, 5 and 7: *Adults & Adolescents (16–80 years of age):* Estrangement from parental figures. Repression and denial related to the unresolved dependency on parental figures. Pseudo-independence. Anxiety in terms of dependency issues. Anger proneness. *Children (8–15 years of age):* Estrangement from parental figures. Pseudo-independence. Anxiety in terms of dependency issues. Anger proneness.
96.	Card A is drawn at least 25% larger than Designs 3, 4, 5 and 7: *Adults & Adolescents (16–80 years of age):* Unresolved dependency on parental figures. Immaturity. Relationship difficulties. *Children (8–15 years of age):* Unresolved dependency on parental figures. Relationship difficulties.

Card 1

97.	Card 1: There are fewer than 12 dots reproduced: *Adults & Adolescents (16–80 years of age):* Tenuous impulse control. Acting out tendencies. Behavioral difficulties. Lack of self criticalness. *Children (8–15 years of age):* Acting out tendencies. Behavioral difficulties. Lack of self-criticalness.
98.	Card 1: There are more than 12 dots reproduced: *All Ages:* Preoccupation with control. Disturbed ideation. Obsessive compulsive functioning.
99.	Card 1: The line of dots extends more than 85% across the width of the page: *Adults & Adolescents (16–80 years of age):* Psychotic preoccupation with control. Requires external, environmental limits on behavior. Acting out likely. *Children (8–15 years of age):* Psychotic preoccupation with control. Acting out likely.
100.	Card 1: The line of dots slopes downward by at least 1/4 inch as compared to a line drawn using a ruler: *All Ages:* Ongoing depression or dysphoria. Self dissatisfaction. Pessimism. Increasing isolation. Consider self-harm possibilities.
101.	Card 1: The line of dots slopes upward by at least 1/4 inch as compared to a line drawn using a ruler: *Adults & Adolescents (16–80 years of age):* Acting out tendencies. Tenuous impulse control. Behavioral and interpersonal difficulties.

(Continued)

Item No.	Distortion and Interpretation

Children (8–15 years of age):
Acting out tendencies. Behavioral and interpersonal difficulties.

102.   Card 1: The slope of the line vacillates. Some dots are drawn at least 1/4 inch above or below the line of dots as compared to a straight line drawn using a ruler, connecting the first and last dots:
Adults & Adolescents (16–80 years of age):
Fluctuating impulse control. Intermittent behavioral dysfunction and interpersonal difficulties. Erratic. Unpredictable. Unreliable.
Children (8–15 years of age):
Intermittent behavioral dysfunction and interpersonal difficulties. Erratic. Unpredictable. Unreliable.

103.   Card 1: There is a change from dots to circles. A circle is any dot wherein you can see a white center:
Adults & Adolescents (16–80 years of age):
Excessive dependency needs. Intense anger or anxiety. Regression in affective functioning. Labile. Histrionic. Prone to exaggeration.
Children (8–15 years of age):
Excessive dependency needs. Intense anger or anxiety. Regression in affective functioning. Labile. Histrionic.

104.   Card 1: At least two dots appear to be drawn as a pair. These dots are spaced closer together (3/8 inch or less) than the others:
Adults & Adolescents (16–80 years of age):
Obsessive-compulsive and paranoid tendencies. Interpersonal difficulties. Lack of empathy.
Children (8–15 years of age):
Paranoid tendencies. Interpersonal difficulties. Lack of empathy.

105.   Card 1: Any spacing between dots which is 3/4 inches or greater:
All Ages:
Possible dissociative episodes.

106.   Card 1: There is visually obvious variability in the shading of the line of dots. Some of the dots in the line are drawn faintly, while other dots are drawn darker than the model. All of the dots are visible:
Adults & Adolescents (16–80 years of age):
Tenuous impulse control. Acting out tendencies. Behavioral difficulties.
Children (8–15 years of age):
Acting out tendencies. Behavioral difficulties.

107.   Card 1: All of the dots in the line are drawn with very dark line quality/ shading:
Adults & Adolescents (16–80 years of age):
Consider sociopathy or psychopathy. Accentuated anger and rage over having to control impulses. Dangerous.
Children (8–15 years of age):
Consider conduct disorder. Accentuated anger and rage over having to control impulses. Dangerous. Explosive.

108.   Card 1: One or more of the dots are drawn with very light shading so as to appear barely visible as compared with the other dots in the design:

(Continued)

Item No.	*Distortion and Interpretation*

Adults & Adolescents (16–80 years of age):
Passive. Dependent. Immature. Submissive. Introverted. Reluctant to express thoughts or feelings. Withholding of emotions. Consider schizoid, inadequate or dependent personality.
Children (8–15 years of age):
Passive. Dependent. Introverted. Reluctant to express thoughts or feelings. Withholding of emotions.

109. Card 1: There is a change from dots to dashes. There are any pencil line dashes or slashes rather than circular dots:
All Ages:
Intense, conscious anger. Exaggerated dependency. Hostility over unmet dependency needs. Excessive impulsivity and aggressivity. (The greater the number of dashes, the more intense and overt the anger.)

110. Card 1 is drawn at least 25% smaller than Designs 2 and 6:
Adults & Adolescents (16–80 years of age):
Tenuous and artificial impulse control. Propensity toward acting out in passiveaggressive and passive-obstructive ways. Feelings of inadequacy and inferiority.
Children (8–15 years of age):
Propensity toward acting out in passive-aggressive and passive-obstructive ways. Feelings of inadequacy and inferiority.

111. Card 1 is drawn at least 25% larger than Designs 2 and 6:
Adults & Adolescents (16–80 years of age):
Inadequate impulse control. Acting out likely. Consider sociopathy; psychopathy; dangerousness; preoccupation with control.
Children (8–15 years of age):
Acting out likely. Consider dangerousness.

Card 2

112. Card 2: Any horizontal row of circles slopes downward by at least 1/4 inch as compared to a line drawn using a ruler:
All Ages:
Conscious self dissatisfaction and self-denigrating behavior; Dysphoria; Anxiety.

113. Card 2: Any horizontal row of circles slopes upward by at least 1/4 inch as compared to a line drawn using a ruler:
All Ages:
Overt, exaggerated expressions of anger. Volatile. Labile. Temperamental.

114. Card 2: There is any decrease in the angulation of any 3-circle column to less than 30 degrees (model has a 45 degree angulation):
All Ages:
Conscious depression. The greater the number of columns that lose angulation to less than 30 degrees, the more severe and chronic the depression. Pessimism. Consider suicidal ideation.

115. Card 2: The first attempt to draw this design results in a reproduction with a row of circles sloping upward by 1/4 inch or greater. This attempt is **erased** and then redrawn correctly:

(*Continued*)

Item No.	Distortion and Interpretation

Adults & Adolescents (16–80 years of age):
Affect driven. Acting out potential. Some ability to self-correct and control inappropriate behavior. Impulsive.
Children (8–15 years of age):
Affect driven. Acting out potential. Some ability to self-correct and control inappropriate behavior.

116. Card 2: The first attempt to draw this design results in a reproduction with a row of circles sloping upward by 1/4 inch or greater. This attempt is **crossed out** and then redrawn correctly:
Adults & Adolescents (16–80 years of age):
Some ability to monitor, self-correct and contain acting-out behavior. Conscious self dissatisfaction. Depression. Impulsivity.
Children (8–15 years of age):
Some ability to monitor, self-correct and contain acting-out behavior. Conscious self dissatisfaction. Depression.

117. Card 2: Any spacing between the columns of circles which is 3/4 inch or greater:
All Ages:
Possible dissociative episodes.

118. Card 2: There are any circles that are closed and colored in (i.e., a change to dots):
All Ages:
Pronounced anger and aggressivity.

119. Card 2: Any column of circles has four or more circles:
All Ages:
Acute schizophrenic or other psychotic processes. Affective and ideational turmoil.

120. Card 2: Any circle is drawn twice the size or greater than the model (1/4″ or greater in diameter):
Adults & Adolescents (16–80 years of age):
Exaggerated dependency. Immaturity. Insecurity.
Children (8–15 years of age):
Exaggerated dependency. Insecurity.

121. Card 2: Any of the lines of any of the circles touch each other:
Adults & Adolescents (16–80 years of age):
Gross dependency. Affective rurmoil. Anger proneness. Immaturity.
Children (8–15 years of age):
Gross dependency. Affective turmoil. Anger proneness.

122. Card 2: The column of circles extends more than 85% across the width of the page:
Adults & Adolescents (16–80 years of age):
Overwhelming depression, possibly to psychotic levels. Consider bi-polar disorder, major depression with psychotic features, exaggerated dependency features. Affect-driven.
Children (8–15 years of age):
Overwhelming depression, possibly to psychotic levels. Consider psychotic features. Affect-driven.

(Continued)

Item No.	Distortion and Interpretation

123. Card 2: There are 8 or fewer columns of circles:
Adults & Adolescents (16–80 years of age):
Conscious constriction of affect; self-dissatisfaction and conscious depression. Tenuous impulse control.
Children (8–15 years of age):
Conscious constriction of affect; self-dissatisfaction and conscious depression.

124. Card 2: There are 12 or more columns of circles:
All Ages:
Affect-driven. Preoccupied with self-dissatisfaction and conscious depression. Perseveration. disturbed ideation.

125. Card 2 is drawn at least 25% smaller than Designs 1 and 6:
All Ages:
Exaggerated dependency strivings that are denied and suppressed. Conscious dissatisfaction. Intense feelings of inadequacy. Anxiety.

126. Card 2 is drawn at least 25% larger than Designs 1 and 6:
All Ages:
Overwhelming depression. Gross dependency features. Intense self-dissatisfaction.

127. Card 2: The first attempt to draw this design results in a reproduction with a row of circles sloping downward by at least 1/4 inch. This is attempt is **crossed out** and then redrawn correctly:
All Ages:
Exaggerated self dissatisfaction. Ongoing depression. Self-harm potential. Ability to self correct and control impulses.

Card 3

128. Card 3: There is a change from dots to circles. A circle is any dot in which you can see a white center:
Adults & Adolescents (16–80 years of age):
Females only: Unresolved dependency on and anger at male/father/ authority figures. Relationship difficulties. Possible identity disturbance.
Males only: Unresolved dependency on and anger at male/father/ authority figures. Selfdissatisfaction. Dysphoria. Possible identity disturbance.
Children (8–15 years of age):
Females only: Unresolved dependency on and anger at male/father/ authority figures.
Males only: Unresolved dependency on and anger at male/father/ authority figures. Self-dissatisfaction. Dysphoria.

129. Card 3: The first attempt at this design is erased or crossed out and then redrawn at least 25% smaller than the first attempt:
Adults & Adolescents (16–80 years of age):
Females only: Fears regarding intimacy. Difficulties with heterosexual functioning. Generalized anxiety. Self-esteem difficulties.

(Continued)

Item No.	Distortion and Interpretation

	Males only: Not adequately separated from mother. Feelings of inadequacy due to problems with potency. Difficulties with heterosexual functioning. Self-esteem difficulties. Generalized anxiety. **Children (8–15 years of age):** *Females only:* Generalized anxiety. Seif-esteem difficulties. *Males only:* Not adequately separated from mother. Self-esteem difficulties. Generalized anxiety.
130.	Card 3: The drawing has more than 16 dots: **All Ages:** Excessive hostility and anger. Aggressive functioning. Dangerousness.
131.	Card 3: The drawing has less than 16 dots: **Adults & Adolescents (16–80 years of age):** Excessive use of denial and repression. Passivity. Avoidance of intimacy; Avoidance of hostility. **Children (8–15 years of age):** Excessive use of denial and repression. Passivity. Avoidance of hostility.
132.	Card 3: There is either more or less than 7 dots in the 7-dot line of the figure: **All Ages:** Excessive anger that would be hidden and denied consciously. Passive aggressive tendencies. Interpersonal difficulties.
133.	Card 3: There is more than 3/4 inch spacing between any of columns of dots. Measure spacing from the center row of dots: **All Ages:** Intense anger reaction that may be denied once controls are reinstated. Dangerous.
134.	Card 3: The center row of dots does not form a straight horizontal line when measured with a ruler. One or more of the dots is 1/4 inch higher or lower than the line of center dots: **Adults & Adolescents only (16–80 years of age):** Possible neurological impairment.
135.	Card 3 is erased or crossed out and redrawn at least 25% shorter or 25% longer (in length) than the model (1 3/8 or smaller; 2 3/8 or greater): **Adults & Adolescents (16–80 years of age):** Anxiety, particularly related to intimacy. Exacerbated dependency features. Self esteem deficits. **Children (8–15 years of age):** Anxiety. Exacerbated dependency features. Self esteem deficits.
136.	Card 3 is drawn more constricted than the model so it measures 1 3/8 inches or less in overall length: **Adults & Adolescents (16–80 years of age):** *Females only:* Suppressed, unresolved anger at father, generalized to males. Passive aggressive tendencies. Self-esteem deficits. Identity disturbance.

(Continued)

Item	*Distortion and Interpretation*
No.	

Males only: Suppressed, unresolved anger at father, generalized to males. Self dissatisfaction. Dysphoria. Self-esteem deficits. Identity disturbance.

Children (8–15 years of age):

Females only: Suppressed, unresolved anger at father, generalized to males. Passive aggressive tendencies. Self-esteem deficits.

Males only: Suppressed, unresolved anger at father, generalized to males. Self dissatisfaction. Dysphoria. Self-esteem deficits.

137. Card 3: There are any dashes instead of dots. There are any pencil line dashes or slashes rather than circular dots:

Adults & Adolescents (16–80 years of age):

Intense hostility in terms of intimacy striving. Excessive impulsivity. Consider the merger of sexual and aggressive behaviors. Dangerous.

Children (8–15 years of age):

Intense hostility. Excessive impulsivity. Dangerous.

138. Card 3 is drawn at least 25% smaller than Designs A, 4, 5 and 7:

Adults & Adolescents (16–80 years of age):

Suppressed affect, particularly assertive and anger affect. Avoidance of intimacy.

Children (8–15 years of age):

Suppressed affect, particularly assertive and anger affect.

139. Card 3 is drawn at least 25% larger than Designs A, 4, 5 and 7:

Adults & Adolescents (16–80 years of age):

Intense overt hostility. Consider sociopathy, psychopathy and the merger of sexual and aggressive behaviors. Dangerous.

Children (8–15 years of age):

Intense overt hostility. Consider conduct disorder and the merger of sexual and aggressive behaviors. Dangerous.

Card 4

140. Card 4: The lines of the square and the curve overlap:

Adults & Adolescents (16–80 years of age):

Females only: Identification with an aggressive male/father figure. Possible identity confusion. Self-loathing. Prone to controlling or verbally/physically abusing males.

Males only: Easily dominated by females. Perceives females as threatening. Passive. Excessively dependent.

Children (8–15 years of age):

Females only: Identification with an aggressive male/father figure. Self-loathing. Prone to controlling or verbally/physically abusing males.

Males only: Perceives females as threatening. Passive. Excessively dependent.

141. Card 4: At least 60% of the curve drawn is placed under the horizontal line of the square as opposed to being drawn intersecting with the square's bottom right corner:

Adults & Adolescents (16–80 years of age):

Females only: Pseudo-seductive. Dysfunctional in intimacy. Role-played and accentuated femininity. Passivity. Relationship difficulties. Anxiety.

(*Continued*)

Item No.	Distortion and Interpretation

Males only: Seeks to verbally or physically abuse females. Identity confused with a manifest need to prove masculinity in accentuated, role-played and pseudo-masculine ways. Promiscuous and frequently homophobic. Relationship difficulties. Anxiety.

Children (8–15 years of age):

Females only: Passivity. Relationship difficulties. Anxiety.

Males only: Seeks to verbally or physically abuse females. Relationship difficulties. Anxiety.

142.　Card 4: At least 60% of the curve drawn is placed adjacent to the right vertical line of the square as opposed to being drawn intersecting with the square's bottom right corner:

Adults & Adolescents (16–80 years of age):

Females only: Intense anger. Intensely competitive with and mistrustful of others, especially females (including children). Difficulty maintaining a supportive role. Disruptive relationships in general.

Males only: Fear of domination by females. Intense anger. Difficulty maintaining intimate relationships and disruptive relationships in general.

Children (8–15 years of age):

Females only: Intense anger. Intensely competitive with and mistrustful of others, especially females (including children). Disruptive relationships in general.

Males only: Fear of domination by females. Intense anger. Disruptive relationships in general.

143.　Card 4: Both corners of the square are more rounded than straight:

Adults & Adolescents (16–80 years of age):

Females only: Feminization and/or minimization of males.

Males only: View themselves and other males negatively. Possible identity disturbance. Self-dissatisfaction.

Children (8–15 years of age):

Females only: Minimization of males.

Males only: View themselves and other males negatively. Self-dissatisfaction.

144.　Card 4: The curved line drawn measures 2 1/2 inches or greater from end to end:

Adults & Adolescents (16–80 years of age):

Females only: Female/mother figure is/was the dominant psychological parent. Enhanced self-esteem and strong role identification.

Males only: Female/mother figure is/was the dominant psychological parent. Possible identity problems. Feelings of inadequacy and self-dissatisfaction.

Children (8–15 years of age):

Females only: Female/mother figure is/was the dominant psychological parent. Enhanced self-esteem.

Males only: Female/mother figure is/was the dominant psychological parent. Feelings of inadequacy and self-dissatisfaction.

(Continued)

Item No.	Distortion and Interpretation

145.   Card 4: The square drawn measures 1 inch or greater at any side:
Adults & Adolescents (16–80 years of age):
Females only: Male/father figure is/was the dominant psychological parent. Possible identity problems and self-dissatisfaction.
Males only: *Male/father figure is/was the dominant psychological parent. Enhanced selfesteem and strong role identification.*
Children (8–15 years of age):
Females only: *Male/father figure is/was the dominant psychological parent. Possible self-dissatisfaction.*
Males only: *Male/father figure is/was the dominant psychological parent. Enhanced selfesteem.*

146.   Card 4: The right vertical side of the box is drawn higher than the left side by at least 1/4 inch:
Adults & Adolescents (16–80 years of age):
Females only: Pseudoseductive. Dysfunctional in intimacy. Role-played and accentuated femininity. Passivity. Relationship difficulties. Anxiety.
Males only: *Seeks to verbally or physically abuse females. Identity confused with a manifest need to prove masculinity in artificial and pseudo-masculine ways. Promiscuous. Homophobic. Chronic relationship difficulties.*
Children (8–15 years of age):
Females only: *Precociousness. Passivity.·Relationship difficulties. Anxiety.*
Males only: *Seeks to verbally or physically abuse females. Chronic relationship difficulties.*

147.   Card 4: The line quality of the square is discernibly darker than that of the curved line:
Adults & Adolescents (16–80 years of age):
Both genders: Accentuated hostility toward males.
Females only: *Pseudoseductive. Dysfunctional with intimacy. Role-playes and accentuated femininity. Passivity; Relationship difficulties. Anxiety.*
Males only: *Seeks to verbally or physically abuse females. Self-dissatisfaction; Identity confused with a manifest need to prove masculinity in pseudomasculine ways. Promiscuous. Relationship difficulties.*
Children (8–15 years of age):
Both genders: Accentuated hostility toward males.
Females only: *Precociousness. Passivity; Relationship difficulties. Anxiety.*
Males only: *Seeks to verbally or physically abuse females. Relationship difficulties.*

148.   Card 4: The figures are completely separated and do not touch at any point:
All Ages:
Severe peer relationship disturbances. Mistrustful. Paranoid. Isolated.

(Continued)

Item No.	Distortion and Interpretation

149.   Card 4: Either or both sides of the square are drawn so that they tilt inward by more than 20 degrees:
    Adults & Adolescents (16–80 years of age):
    <u>Both Genders</u>: *Emotionally constricted, rejecting and ungiving male/ father figure.*
    <u>Females only</u>: *Relationship disturbances. Anxiety. Difficulties with intimacy.*
    <u>Males only</u>: *Self-dissatisfaction. Feelings of inadequacy. Possible identity disturbance. Depression. Dysthymia.*
    Children (8–15 years of age):
    <u>Both Genders</u>: *Emotionally constricted, rejecting and ungiving male/ father figure.*
    <u>Females only</u>: *Relationship disturbances. Anxiety.*
    <u>Males only</u>: *Self-dissatisfaction. Feelings of inadequacy. Depression. Dysthymia.*

150.   Card 4: Either or both sides of the curved shape are drawn so that they tilt inward by more than 20 degrees:
    Adults & Adolescents (16–80 years of age):
    <u>Both Genders</u>: *Emotionally constricted, rejecting and ungiving female/mother figure.*
    <u>Females only</u>: *Self-dissatisfaction. Feelings of inadequacy. Possible identity disturbance. Depression.*
    <u>Males only</u>: *Relationship disturbances. Anxiety. Difficulties with intimacy.*
    Children (8–15 years of age):
    <u>Both Genders</u>: *Emotionally constricted, rejecting and ungiving female/mother figure.*
    <u>Females only</u>: *Self-dissatisfaction. Feelings of inadequacy. Depression.*
    <u>Males only</u>: *Relationship disturbances. Anxiety.*

151.   Card 4 is drawn at least 25% smaller than Designs A, 3, 5 and 7:
    Adults & Adolescents (16–80 years of age):
    Disturbance of peer-relationships. Intense anxiety. Passivity. Covert dependency features. Immaturity.
    Children (8–15 years of age):
    Disturbance of peer-relationships. Intense anxiety. Passivity. Covert dependency features.

152.   Card 4 is drawn at least 25% larger than Designs A, 3, 5 and 7:
    Adults & Adolescents (16–80 years of age):
    Intense anger toward parental and authority figures. Severe peer relationship disturbances. Extreme dependency and immaturity. Acting out tendencies likely.
    Children (8–15 years of age):
    Intense anger toward parental and authority figures. Severe peer relationship disturbances. Extreme dependency. Acting out tendencies likely.

(Continued)

Item No.	*Distortion and Interpretation*

Card 5

153. Card 5: The design is drawn with less than seven dots in the straight row of dots:
      Adults & Adolescents (16–80 years of age):
      <u>Females only</u>: *Identifies with aggressive father figure. Unresolved anger at father which generalized to males in positions of authority. Volatile. Denigrating of males. Possible identity concerns. Possible trauma.*
      Males only: *Inadequate separation from mother. Feelings of inadequacy. Difficulties with intimacy. Self-esteem difficulties. Dependency.*
      Children (8–15 years of age):
      <u>Females only</u>: *Identifies with aggressive father figure. Unresolved anger at father which generalized to males in positions of authority. Volatile. Denigrating of males. Possible trauma.*
      <u>Males only</u>: *Inadequate separation from mother. Feelings of inadequacy. Self-esteem difficulties. Dependency.*

154. Card 5: The first dot on the left-hand side of the arch is missing and/or the arch is drawn lopsided, giving the appearance that the first dot is missing:
      Adults & Adolescents (16–80 years of age):
      Inadequate bonding with mother/female figure. Inadequate nurturance from mother/female during infancy. Accentuated dependency due to unmet needs for nurture. Consider schizophrenia, bipolar disorder, other forms of psychosis, and borderline states. Addiction-proneness. Eating disorders.
      Children (8–15 years of age):
      Inadequate bonding with mother/female figure. Inadequate nurturance from mother/female during infancy. Accentuated dependency due to unmet needs for nurture. Consider schizophrenia, bipolar disorder and other forms of psychosis. Addictionproneness. Eating disorders.

155. Card 5: There is 1/4 inch or more separation between any of the dots of the curved figure.
      All Ages:
      (Counting from left to right, each dot represents 1 successive year from ages 1–19): A large separation between dors indicares rhe approximate age at which separation from mother/female nurturing figure was traumatic. Anxiety. Depression. Relationship difficulties. Dependency. Self-esteem difficulties.

156. Card 5: There is any change from dots to circles. A circle is any dot in which you can see a white center. The higher the number of circles, the greater the degree of disturbance:
      Adults & Adolescents (16–80 years of age):
      Exacerbated dependency processes and excessive demand for nurture due to neglect and nurture deprivation. Immaturity. Consider addiction-proneness. Possible psychosis, psychopathy, sociopathy and borderline states.

(Continued)

Item No.	Distortion and Interpretation

<u>Children (8–15 years of age):</u>
Exacerbated dependency processes and excessive demand for nurture due to neglect and nurture deprivation. Consider addiction-proneness. Possible psychosis and conduct disorder.

157. Card 5: The intersection of the straight row of dots and the arch deviates, so that it is no longer between the eleventh and twelfth dots (counting from left to right):
<u>Ages 13 and older:</u>
The age at which there was possible delay or precociousness with regard to the onset of puberty. Possible physical, sexual or psychological trauma at that age.

158. Card 5: There are any pencil line dashes or slashes instead of circular dots used for either or both figures:
<u>Adults & Adolescents (16–80 years of age):</u>
Exaggerated dependency. Immaturity. Avoidance of intimacy. Accentuated anger. Consider anorexia.
<u>Children (8–15 years of age):</u>
Exaggerated dependency. Accentuated anger. Consider anorexia.

159. Card 5: There is any significant rotation of this design:
<u>All Ages:</u>
Neurologic impairment. Affective turmoil. Atypical or deviant dependency needs. Significant interpersonal difficulties.

160. Card 5: The design is drawn with more than 7 dots on the straight row of dots:
<u>Adults & Adolescents (16–80 years of age):</u>
Females only: Perception of males as dangerous. Fear of heterosexual functioning. Possible trauma.
Males only: Self-perception as aggressive. Merger of sexual and aggressive behavior. Dangerousness. Pseudomasculine.
<u>Children (8–15 years of age):</u>
Females only: Perceprion of males as dangerous. Possible trauma.
Males only: Self-perception as aggressive. Dangerousness.

161. Card 5: Any of the dots in the straight row of dots is drawn visibly fainter than those of the semi circle:
<u>Adults & Adolescents (16–80 years of age):</u>
Unresolved anger at father/male authority figures. Fear of intimacy. Possible sexual trauma. Immaturity. Passivity.
<u>Children (8–15 years of age):</u>
Unresolved anger at father/male authority figures. Possible sexual trauma. Passivity.

162. Card 5 is drawn at least 25% smaller than Designs A, 3, 4 and 7:
<u>Ages 13 and older:</u>
Difficulties with the onset of puberty. Anxiety. Dependency. Constricted affective functioning. Self dissatisfaction. Feelings of inadequacy. Withdrawal. Passivity.

(Continued)

Item No.	Distortion and Interpretation

163.   Card 5 is drawn at least 25% larger than Designs Λ, 3, 4 and 7:
Adults & Adolescents (16–80 years of age):
Exaggerated dependency. Preoccupation with intimacy ideations. Immaturity. Selfdissatisfaction. Possible psychosis.
Children (8–15 years of age):
Exaggerated dependency. Preoccupation with intimacy ideations. Self-dissatisfaction. Possible psychosis.

Card 6

164.   Card 6: Compared to the intersection of the model, the vertical line drawn intersects the horizontal line towards the right and a majority of the vertical line is below the horizontal line (at least 1/2 inch out and 1/2 inch down):
All Ages:
Severe depression, possibly to psychotic levels.

165.   Card 6: Compared to the intersection of the model, the vertical line drawn intersects the horizontal line towards the right and a majority of the vertical line is above the horizontal line (at least 1/2 inch out and 1/2 inch up):
Adults & Adolescents (16–80 years of age):
Acting out tendencies. Poor impulse control. Affective turmoil. Impaired self- concept. Consider conduct or personality disorder.
Children (8–15 years of age):
Acting out tendencies. Affective turmoil. Impaired self-concept. Consider conduct disorder.

166.   Card 6: Compared to the intersection of the model, the vertical line drawn intersects the horizontal line towards the left and a majority of the vertical line is below the horizontal line (at least 1/2 inch in and 1/2 inch down):
Adults & Adolescents (16–80 years of age):
Affect driven. Dependency. Anger prone. Forgetful. Histrionic. Impulsive.
Children (8–15 years of age):
Affect driven. Anger prone. Forgetful. Histrionic.

167.   Card 6: Compared to the intersection of the model, the vertical line drawn intersects the horizontal line towards the left and a majority of the vertical line is above the horizontal line (at least 1/2 inch in and 1 /2 inch up):
All Ages:
Severe depression. Consider suicide or homicide potential. Acting out tendencies.

168.   Card 6: The horizontal line ascends by at least 20 degrees as compared to a straight line drawn using a ruler:
Adults & Adolescents (16–80 years of age):
Acting out tendencies. Affective turmoil. Tenuous impulse control. Consider sociopathy, borderline states, psychopathy and addiction-proneness.
Children (8–15 years of age):
Acting out tendencies. Affective turmoil. Consider conduct disorder, borderline states, and addiction-proneness.

(Continued)

Item No.	*Distortion and Interpretation*
169.	Card 6: The horizontal line descends by at least 20 degrees as compared to a straight line drawn using a ruler: ***All Ages:*** *Exaggerated dysphoric tendencies. Depression.*
170.	Card 6: The horizontal line is discernibly lighter than the vertical line: ***All Ages:*** *Suppression of affect. Passivity. Stoicism.*
171.	Card 6: The horizontal line is discernibly darker than the vertical line: ***Adults & Adolescents (16–80 years of age):*** *Affect driven. Hostile. Labile. Potentially dangerous. Consider bipolar disorder, borderline personality disorder and anti-social personality disorder.* ***Children (8–15 years of age):*** *Affect driven. Hostile. Labile. Potentially dangerous. Consider bipolar disorder, borderline and conduct disorder.*
172.	Card 6: Any curves are squared off (pointed) on either or both lines: ***All Ages:*** *Neurological impairment.*
173.	Card 6: There are any erasures on the horizontal line: ***Adults & Adolescents (16–80 years of age):*** *Accentuated affect. Affective turmoil. Anxiety. Consider bi-polar disorder, schizoaffective disorder and borderline personality disorder.* ***Children (8–15 years of age):*** *Accentuated affect. Affective turmoil. Anxiety. Consider bi-polar disorder, schizoaffective disorder and borderline states.*
174.	Card 6: There are any erasures on the vertical line: ***All Ages:*** *Accentuated hostility, either overt or passive-aggressive. Anger prone.*
175.	Card 6: The angle of the vertical line deviates by more than 20 degrees in either direction from the model: ***All Ages:*** *Excessive hostility. Anger prone.*
176.	Card 6: The angle of the vertical line deviates by more than 50 degrees to the left as compared to the model: ***Adults & Adolescents (16–80 years of (age):*** *Rebelliousness and negativism. Intense anger. Consider acute distress, conduct disorder, borderline, sociopathy and psychopathy.* ***Children (8–15 years of age):*** *Rebelliousness and negativism. Intense anger. Consider acute distress, conduct disorder, and borderline states.*
177.	Card 6: There are projecting lines on the vertical line above its intersection with the horizontal line: ***All Ages:*** *Excessive expressed hostility. Anger prone.*
178.	Card 6: There are projecting lines on the vertical line below its intersection with the horizontal line: ***All Ages:*** *Excessive use of repression and denial of hostility.*

(Continued)

Item No.	Distortion and Interpretation

179. Card 6: There are projecting lines on the horizontal line to the left of the vertical line:
All Ages:
Feelings of self-dissatisfaction. Dysthymia. Depression. Consider self-harm potential.

180. Card 6: There are projecting lines on the horizontal line to the right of the vertical line:
Adults & Adolescents (16–80 years of age):
Displaced anger. Hyper-criticalness of others. Projection. Lack of insight.
Children (8–15 years of age):
Displaced anger. Hyper-criticalness of others. Lack of insight.

181. Card 6: There are additional curves on the vertical line:
All Ages:
Accentuated verbal or physical hostility. Aggressivity. Dangerous.

182. Card 6: The horizontal line has 3 or fewer complete curves:
Adults & Adolescents (16–80 years of age):
Repression of affective functioning. Stoicism. Lack of empathy; possible neurologic deficits; Impulsivity, lack of self-criticalness.
Children (8–15 years of age):
Repression of affective functioning. Stoicism. Lack of empathy; possible neurologic deficits; Lack of self-criticalness.

183. Card 6 is drawn at least 25% smaller than Designs 1 and 2:
All Ages:
Repression of affective functioning. Stoicism. Lack of empathy.

184. Card 6 is drawn at least 25% larger than Designs 1 and 2:
Adults & Adolescents (16–80 years of age):
Affect driven. Lack of self-criticalness. Intense hostility. Dangerousness. Consider sociopathy, psychopathy, borderline personality, and psychosis.
Children (8–15 years of age):
Affect driven. Lack of self-criticalness. Intense hostility. Dangerousness. Consider conduct disorder, borderline states and psychosis.

185. Card 6: The horizontal line has 5 or more curves:
Adults & Adolescents (16–80 years of age):
Affect driven. Immaturity. Poor impulse control. Lack of self-criticalness.
Children (8–15 years of age):
Affect driven. Poor impulse control. Lack of self-criticalness.

Card 7

186. Card 7: There is any loss of angulation, flattening of figures or rounding of comers:
All Ages:
Possible neurological impairment.

(*Continued*)

Item No.	Distortion and Interpretation

187. Card 7: There are any broken lines:
Adults & Adolescents (16–80 years of age):
*Possible neurological impairment. Aversion to intimacy. Difficulties
in sexual and intimate functioning.*
Children (8–15 years of age):
Difficulties in interpersonal relations.

188. Card 7: The figures do not overlap at all or overlap insufficiently, in
that less than 1/8 inch or less of the figures overlap at their widest point:
Adults & Adolescents (16–80 years of age):
*Overwhelming fear of intimacy. Generalized anxiety. Chronic
relationship difficulties.*
Children (8–15 years of age):
Generalized anxiety. Chronic relationship difficulties.

189. Card 7: The figures overlap excessively in that more than 3/8 inch of
either figure overlaps at its widest point:
Adults & Adolescents (16–80 years of age):
*Preoccupation with intimacy-related ideation. Consider psychotic
processes. Regression. Ideational turmoil.*
Children (8–15 years of age):
Consider psychotic processes. Regression.

190. Card 7: Either or both figures is drawn significantly larger or smaller
than the model (larger = > 2″ in height or > 3/4″ in width; smaller = < 1
1/4″ height or < 3/8″ in width:
Adults & Adolescents (16–80 years of age):
*Exaggerated sexual ideation. There is the likelihood of sexual acting
out. Dangerous. Immature. Consider psychosis, sexual predator,
pedophilia, or sociopathy.*
Children (8–15 years of age):
*Exaggerated sexual ideation. There is the likelihood of sexual acting
out. Dangerous. Immature. Consider psychosis, sexual predator,
pedophilia, or a conduct disorder.*

191. Card 7: There are any erasures:
Adults & Adolescents (16–80 years of age):
Anxiery regarding intimate functioning. Possible sexual trauma.
Children (8–15 years of age):
Anxiety. Possible trauma.

192. Card 7: Either or both figures is completely erased and redrawn:
Adults & Adolescents (16–80 years of age):
*Extreme aversion to intimacy. Ideational turmoil. Regression.
Possible psychosis. Chronic anxiety. Consider trauma.*
Children (8–15 years of age):
*Ideational turmoil. Regression. Possible psychosis. Chronic anxiety.
Consider trauma.*

193. Card 7: Any corners are discernibly sharper/darker than any
others:
All Ages:
*Aggressive tendencies. Merger of sexual and aggressive behavior.
Possible sexual trauma. Violence prone.*

(Continued)

Item No.	Distortion and Interpretation

194. Card 7: There is inconsistent line quality. The line quality vacillates between dark and faint lines:
All Ages:
Possible trauma. Anger-prone. Relationship difficulties.

195. Card 7 is drawn at least 25% smaller than Designs A, 3, 4 and 5:
Adults & Adolescents (16–80 years of age):
Intense anxiety related to intimacy. Anhedonia. Immaturity. Superficial and transient relationships.
Children (8–15 years of age):
Intense anxiety. Anhedonia.

196. Card 7 is drawn at least 25% larger than Designs A, 3, 4 and 5:
Adults & Adolescents (16–80 years of age):
Gross dysfunction with intimacy. Sexual acting out likely. Possible sexual trauma. Consider dangerousness.
Children (8–15 years of age):
Sexual acting out likely. Possible sexual trauma. Consider dangerousness.

197. Card 7: Any change of angulation in which any angle of either or both figures differs more than 20 degrees(+/-) from those of the model:
All Ages:
Possible neurologic deficits.

Card 8

198. Card 8: The length of the outer shape is 2 1/4 inches or less:
Adults & Adolescents (16–80 years of age):
Females only: *Conscious avoidance of intimacy. Consider physical or sexual trauma. Possible identity disturbance.*
Males only: *Feelings of inadequacy. Conscious avoidance of intimacy. Possible identity disturbance. Consider trauma.*
Children (8–15 years of age):
Females only: *Consider physical or sexual trauma.*
Males only: *Feelings of inadequacy. Consider trauma.*

199. Card 8: Any of the lines of the center diamond extend beyond the lines of the outer shape:
Adults & Adolescents (16–80 years of age):
Females only: Disinterest, dislike and/or avoidance of intimacy.
Males only: *Preoccupation with intimacy ideation. Sexual acting out. Poor impulse control. Dangerousness.*
Children (8–15 years of age):
Females only: *Consider trauma.*
Males only: *Preoccupation with intimacy ideation. Sexual acting out. Dangerousness.*

200. Card 8: There are any broken lines or lines that do not meet at the end points:
Adults & Adolescents (16–80 years of age):
Possible trauma. Immaturity. Merger of sexual and aggressive behaviors. Ideational turmoil.

(Continued)

Item No.	Distortion and Interpretation
	Children (8–15 years of age): *Possible trauma. Aggressive behaviors. Ideational turmoil.*
201.	Card 8 is drawn at least 3 1/2 inches in length and at least 1 inch in height: **Adults & Adolescents (16–80 years of age):** *Preoccupation with intimacy. Consider merger of sexual and aggressive behavior. Possible psychotic processes. Acting out. Dangerous.* **Children (8–15 years of age):** *Consider merger of sexual and aggressive behavior. Possible psychotic processes. Acting out. Dangerous.*
202.	Card 8: The lines of the outer shape are wavy and vacillate from a straight line by more than 1/8 inch in either direction: **Adults & Adolescents (16–80 years of age):** *Low frustration tolerance. Self-denigration. Tenuous impulse control.* **Children (8–15 years of age):** *Low frustration tolerance. Self-denigration. Acting out tendencies.*
203.	Card 8 is drawn at least 3 1/2 inches in length and the height of the design is drawn comparable to the height of the model (1/2 inch): **Adults & Adolescents (16–80 years of age):** *Preoccupation with intimacy. Overlap of sexual and aggressive behavior.* **Children (8–15 years of age):** *Inappropriate and merged sexual and aggressive behavior.*
204.	Card 8: Any lines are discernibly lighter than others; Any faint lines: **Adults & Adolescents (16–80 years of age):** *Anxiety. Fear of intimacy. Possible trauma. Passivity.* **Children (8–15 years of age):** *Anxiety. Possible trauma. Passivity.*
205.	Card 8: Any lines or corners are discernibly darker and/or there are sharpened angles: **Adults & Adolescents (16–80 years of age):** *Aggressive tendencies. Merger of sexual and aggressive behavior. Possible sexual trauma. Violence prone.* **Children (8–15 years of age):** *Aggressive tendencies. Possible trauma. Violence prone.*
206.	Card 8: There are any rounded and/or flattened corners: **All Ages:** *Consider neurological impairment*
207.	Design 8 is 25% longer than any other design: **Adults & Adolescents (16–80 years of age):** *Gross dysfunction with intimacy. Sexual acting out. Possible sexual trauma. Dangerousness. Severe aggressive ideation.* **Children (8–15 years of age):** *Inappropriate sexual acting out. Possible trauma. Dangerousness. Severe aggressive ideation.*

(Continued)

Item No.	*Distortion and Interpretation*

Experimental Items:

E1. A Design or component of any design is omitted.
All Ages:
Anxiety reaction to the design in question; Significantly accentuates the importance of the interpretations of that design.

E2. Any design is drawn on a separate page from all others.
All Ages:
Anxiety reaction to the design in question; Accentuates the importance of the interpretations of that design.

E3. Any erasures on any design where improvement does not occur.
All Ages:
Anxiety reaction to the design in question; Accentuates the importance of the interpretation of that design.

E 4. Any attempt at any design is crossed out.
All Ages:
Increased anger and ambivalence toward the psychological issues measured by that design.

E5. All of the designs are drawn in the bottom half of the page.
Adults & Adolescents (16–80 years of age):
Possible administration error. Concreteness, poor planning; possible depression; dysthmia; dependency; immaturity.
Children (8–15 years of age):
Possible administration error. Concreteness, poor planning; possible depression; dysthmia.

E6. Significant rotation of any design:
All Ages:
Consider neurologic and perceptual motor deficits; use a second administration and further testing to rule out.

E7. A majority of the designs are drawn with dark shading
Adults & Adolescents (16–80 years of age):
Check the type of pencil used (should be #2); If pencil is not causal, consider sociopathy, psychopathy; accentuated anger and hostility.
Children (8–15 years of age):
Check the type of pencil used (should be #2); If pencil is not causal, consider conduct disorder; accentuated anger and hostility.

E8. There are any embellishment or additions of new components to a design.
Adults & Adolescents (16–80 years of age):
Histrionic. Reflects affect deprivation; dependency; possible manic quality (seen in individuals currently in the mania stage of bi-polar disorder). Evasive. Immature.
Children (8–15 years of age):
Histrionic. Reflects affect deprivation; dependency

E9. Card 3: Any vertical line within the arrow loses its angularity (e.g., straightened/flattened).
Adults & Adolescents (16–80 years of age):
Possible neurologic deficit; possible impulsiviry; depression,·heightened aggressivity.

(Continued)

Item No.	*Distortion and Interpretation*

Children (8–15 years of age):
Possible neurologic deficit; Depression; heightened aggressivity.

E10.   Card 4: The line quality of the curved line is discernibly darker than that of the square:
Adults & Adolescents (16–80 years of age):
Both genders: Accentuated hostility toward females.
Females only: Seeks to verbally or physically abuse males. Self-dissatisfaction; Identity confused with a manifest need to prove femininity in pseudofeminine ways. Promiscuous. Relationship difficulties.
Males only: Pseudoseductive. Dysfunctional with intimacy. Role-played and accentuated masculinity. Relationship difficulties. Anxiety.
Children (8–15 years of age):
Both genders: Accentuated hostility toward females.
Females only: Seeks to verbally or physically abuse males. Self-dissatisfaction; Relationship difficulties.
Males only: Precocious. Relationship difficulties. Anxiety.

E11.   Card 6: The vertical line has less than 3 complete curves:
Adults & Adolescents (16–80 years of age):
Suppressed anger; passivity; passive-aggressive behavior; possible neurologic deficits. Impulsive; Lacks self-criticalness. Role-playing.
Children (8–15 years of age):
Suppressed anger; passivity; passive-aggressive behavior; possible neurologic deficits. Lacks self-criticalness.

Appendix G
Bender Gestalt Test – Advanced Interpretation Scoring Key

Name/ID: _____ Date: _____ Gender: Age: _____

Score as 1 point unless specified as a (2) or (5). Distortions may be in one or more category. Consider Major Mental Illness (e.g., Psychosis, Schizophrenia, Bi-Polars):

2 (5)	15. (5)	25. (5)	37. (5)	51.	(5)	122. (5)	173. (5)
7.	16. (5)	26. (5)	38. (5)	52.	(5)	154.	184. (5)
9. (5)	17. (5)	29. (5)	39. (5)	53.	(5)	156. (2)	189. (5)
10. (5)	18. (5)	30. (5)	40. (5)	54.	(5)	163.	190.
11. (5)	19. (5)	32. (5)	44. (5)	55.	(5)	164. (5)	192. (5)
12. (5)	20. (5)	33. (5)	45. (5)	76.	(5)	167. (5)	207. (5)
13. (5)	21. (5)	34. (5)	47. (5)	99.	(5)	168. (5)	
14. (5)	22. (5)	36. (5)	49. (5)	119. (5)	171. (5)		

Consider Mild to Moderate Personality Deficits (e.g., Axis I and Axis Il}):

1. (2)	61.	86.		I 12.	138.	165. (2)	199. (2)
4.	61.	87.	(2)	113.	139. (2)	166.	200. (2)
5.	63.	88.	(2)	114.	140.	169.	201. (2)
6.	64.	89.		115. (2)	141.	170.	202. (2)
7.	65.	90.		116.	142.	174.	203. (2)
8. (2)	66. (2)	91.		117. (2)	143.	175.	204.
23. (2)	67. (2)	92.		118.	144.	176. (2)	205. (2)
24. (2)	68. (2)	95.		120.	145.	177.	
27. (2)	69. (2)	96.		121.	146.	178.	
28. (2)	70. (2)	97. (2)		123. (2)	147.	179.	
31. (2)	71. (2)	98. (2)		124. (2)	148. (2)	180.	
35. (2)	72. (2)	100.		125.	149.	181. (2)	
41. (2)	73.	101. (2)		126.	150.	182. (2)	
42. (2)	74. (2)	102.		127. (2)	151.	183.	
43. (2)	75. (2)	103.		128.	152. (2)	185.	
46. (2)	77.	104. (2)		129.	153.	187.	

48.	(2)	78.	105. (2)	130. (2)	155.	188. (2)
50.	(2)	80.	106. (2)	131.	157.	191.
56.	(2)	81.	107. (2)	132.	158. (2)	193. (2)
57.		82.	108.	133. (2)	159. (2)	194.
58.		83.	109.	135.	160. (2)	195.
59.	(2)	84.	110.	136.	161.	196. (2)
60.		85.	111. (2)	137. (2)	162.	198.

Consider Organic, Neurologic. Deficits:

3.	34.	52.	56.		159. (3)	197. (3)
7.	40.	53.	93.	(3)	172. (3)	206.
19.	41.	54.	94.	(3)	186. (3)	
27.	45.	55.	134.	(3)	187.	

_____Total Points For Section I. Major Mental Illness Indicators
_____Total Points For Section II. Moderate Personality Deficits Indicators
_____Total Points For Section III. Neurologic Deficits Indicators
_____Total Points For all 3 Sections.

Consider Major Mental Illness and/or Organicity if any subscale measures as follows:

Section I (MMI) – Major Mental Illness Score = 21 and greater
Section II (MPI) – Moderate Personality Deficit Score = 34 and greater
Total Score = 63 and greater

Consider Moderate Personality Deficits (Axis I and II) if there are no scores in the Major Mental Illness range and any subscale measures as follows:

Section I – Major Mental Illness Score = 12–20
Section II – Moderate Personality Deficit Score = 29–33
Total Score = 47–61

Consider Brain Injury if the BI score is >8 and neither the MMI > 12 and MPI > 29. If BI is elevated along with MMI, consider the possibility of cognitive and personality problems being present simultaneously.

References

Aucone, E. J., Raphael, A. J., Golden, C. J., Espe-Pfeifer, P., Seldon, J., Pospisil, T., Dornheim, L., Proctor-Weber, Z., & Calabria, M. (1999). Reliability of the Advanced Psychodiagnostic Interpretation (API) scoring system for the Bender Gestalt. *Assessment*, *68*(3), 301–303.

Aucone, E. J., Wagner, E. E., Raphael, A. J., Golden, C. J., Espe-Pfeifer, P., Dornheim, L., Seldon, J., Pospisil, T., Proctor-Weber, Z., & Calabria, M. (2001). Test-retest reliability of the Advanced Psychodiagnostic Interpretation (API) scoring system for the Bender Gestalt in chronic schizophrenics. *Assessment*, *8*(3), 351–353.

Buck, J. N. (1948a). The H-T-P test. *Journal of Clinical Psychology*, *4*(2), 151–159.

Buck, J. N. (1948b). The H-T-P technique, a qualitative and quantitative scoring method. *Journal of Clinical Psychology Monographs Supplement*, *5*, 1–120.

Burns, R. C., & Kaufman, S. H. (1970). *Kinetic Family Drawings (K-F-D): An introduction to understanding children through Kinetic Drawings*. New York: Brunner/Mazel, Inc.

Burns, R. C., & Kaufman, S. H. (1972). *Actions, styles and symbols in Kinetic Family Drawings (K-F-D): An interpretive manual*. New York: Brunner/Mazel, Inc.

Freud, S. (1912-1913). *Totem and Taboo*. Translated. New York: Moffatt, Yard, 1919.

Gillespie, J. (1994). *The projective use of Mother-and-Child Drawings: A manual for clinicians*. New York: Brunner/Mazel, Inc.

Goodenough, F. (1926). *Measurement of intelligence by drawings*. New York: World Book Company.

Groth-Marnat, G. (2003). *Handbook of psychological assessment* (4th ed.). Hoboken, NJ: John Wiley & Sons, Inc.

Handler, L., & Thomas, A. D., (Eds.). (2014). *Drawings in assessment and psychotherapy: Research and application*. New York, NY: Routledge.

Killian, G. A. (1984). The House-Tree-Person Technique. In Keyser, D. and Sweetland, R. (Eds.), *Test Critiques*, Vol. I, Kansas City, MO: Test Corporation of America, 338–353.

Koppitz, E. M. (1968). *Psychological evaluation of children's human figure drawings*. Needham Heights, MA: Allyn and Bacon.

Koppitz, E. M. (1984). *Psychological evaluation of human figure drawings by middle school pupils*. Needham Heights, MA: Allyn and Bacon.

Le Corff, Y., Tivendell, J., & LeBlanc, C. (2014). The tree test: a parsimonious projective drawing technique. In L. Handler & A. D. Thomas (Eds.), *Drawings in Assessment and Psychotherapy*. New York, NY: Routledge.

Machover, K. (1949). *Personality projection in the drawing of the human figure: A method of personality investigation*. Springfield, IL: Charles C. Thomas.

Miller, R. L., Paolino, A. M., Ascheman Jones, T., Raphael, A. J., & Golden, C. J. (2018). Inter-rater reliability of the Raphael Projective System (RPS) of Scoring Projective Drawings. *Archives of Assessment Psychology, 8*(1), 57–65.

Naglieri, J. A. (1988). *Draw A Person: A quantitative scoring system*. San Antonio, TX: Psychological Corporation.

Naglieri, J. A., McNeish, T. J., & Bardos, A. N. (1991). *DAP: SPED: Draw A Person: Screening procedure for emotional disturbance: Examiner's manual*. Austin, TX: Pro-Ed, Inc.

Phillips, L., & Smith, Ph.D. (1953). *Rorschach interpretation: Advanced technique*. New York NY: Grune & Stratton.

Rapaport, D., Gill, M. M., & Schafer, R. (1968). *Diagnostic psychological testing*. R. R. Holt (Ed.). New York, NY: International Universities Press, Inc.

Raphael, A. J., & Golden, C. J. (2002). Relationships of objectively scored Bender variables with MMPI scores in an outpatient psychiatric population. *Perceptual and Motor Skills, 95*(3), 1217–1232.

Raphael, A. J., Golden, C., & Raphael, M. A. (2012). *The Advanced Scoring System forthe Bender Gestalt Test- Revised (ABGT-R): Ages 8-80*. Deer Park, NY: Linus Publications, Inc.

Reichenberg, N., & Raphael, A. J. (1992). *Advanced Psychodiagnostic interpretation of the Bender Gestalt Test: Adults and children*. New York, NY: Praeger Publishers.

Smith, J., Gacono, C., Fontan, P., Cunliffe, T., & Andronikof, A. (2020). Understanding Rorschach Research: Using the Mihura (2019) Commentary as a Reference. 27. 71–82.

Van Hutton, V. (1994). *House-Tree-Person and Draw-A-Person as measures of abuse in children: A quantitative scoring system*. Odessa, FL: Psychological Assessment Resources, Inc.

Index

Note: Page numbers followed by "n" refer to notes; and page numbers in **Bold** refer to tables; and page numbers in *italics* refer to figures